Chaos To Clarity™

How to get out of your own way and remember what really matters

Simon
X

TheSimpleidea™

First Published 2023

Published by The Simple Idea Ltd. (www.TheSimpleIdea.com)

DISCLAIMER:

The information and content provided in this book are for general informational purposes only. This book has been produced on a best-efforts basis. The author and publisher have made every effort to ensure the accuracy of the information presented herein, but they do not guarantee or warrant the completeness, adequacy, or currency of the content. Readers should consult with appropriate professionals or experts in specific areas if they require personalized advice or assistance. Explicitly this book does not constitute professional advice. You are recommended to consult with your local medical, mental health, accounting, legal and other relevant regulatory approved professionals as relevant to your circumstances and legal jurisdiction.

The author and publisher shall have no liability for any loss, injury, or damages arising from the use or reliance on the information contained in this book. They disclaim all responsibility for any errors or omissions in the content. Additionally, the author and publisher do not assume any responsibility or liability for third-party content linked to or referenced in this book.

Any resemblance to actual persons, living or dead, or events is purely coincidental.

By reading this book, you acknowledge and agree to the terms of this disclaimer. If you do not agree with these terms, you should not read or use this book.

This book is dedicated to those who care more about people and doing what really matters.

Simon Hedley is a 'Must have' on your speed dial.
Simon connects people with the 'unconnectable.'

— **Idea Mensch**
Where Entrepreneurs Teach Entrepreneurs

It is refreshing indeed to have an honest and real exploration of the inner landscape, rather than outer-referenced theoretical proscriptions. Gratitude and thanks to Simon for this superb offering.

— **Terry Stout, MsD**

Simon's distinctions helped me in a time of complete chaos, I moved to a greater clarity in my life & am now building businesses with legacy. This is the book for people who want to navigate this turbulent time as paradigms shift, and who want to learn to ride and dance with it. Chaos to Clarity helps you get set for just that.

— **Rachel Sheila Kan**
Ecosystem Architect

In a world constantly evolving with technology and AI, this book provides an invaluable perspective on embracing the uncertainties of learning, unlocking hidden potentials, and finding our own unique path to mastery. If you want to become a better at everything you do and unlock the power of a beginner's mindset, I highly recommend Chaos to Clarity. It has the power to change the way you approach learning and, ultimately, your life.

— **Safaraz Ali**
CEO, Founder of Pathway Group

This book will equip you with the tools to get clear on what matters most and show you how to build your life around those answers.

— Simon Alexander Ong

International Keynote Speaker, Bestselling Author of Energize

Simon is the most intelligent and creative man I know. He enables people to give birth to their vision underpinned by being a wizard with technology. Simon is very connected with a huge heart and is tenacious in his approach, that makes the difference. Simon is a genius.

Life is going to get more and more challenging over the next few years and when people have had enough, more and more people will want to find their way and discover the incremental steps to take. Chaos to Clarity couldn't have come a better time.

— Dr Neslyn Watson-Druée CBE

A 30-minute conversation with Simon could save you countless hours and money going round in circles. He'll quickly uncover a pathway to clarity and results.

—Joe Gregory

Award Winning Author & Publisher

Simon has an excellent ability to see the bigger picture and connect the dots to get there. He has wonderful rapport and is incredibly generous with his ideas and thinking. My perspective has shifted through working with him. Simon brings so much more to the table that you initially think. If you're up to something big then Simon will help you get there.

— Cathy Burke

Author, Speaker & Change Maker

Simon is a natural, intuitive synthesizer with the power to transform things for the better. In 'Chaos to Clarity' his strategic alchemy gently but firmly guides you to discern what really matters to you, leading you towards becoming who you are meant to be.

— Ken Alston
Circularity Professional

I have always loved chaos. I know that's where my best ideas are born. But I can get stuck in the chaos phase and never get to that clarity part. Simon Hedley effectively bridged the gap between the chaos I love and the clarity I often found elusive. The chaos where my best ideas were born found a companion in this book, a guide to channel it productively. The Key Questions at the end of each chapter served as reflective pauses for me, enabling an intimate dialogue with my thoughts. The Thought Experiments scattered throughout became my gateway to deeper introspection. Most strikingly, the question, "Do I know what really matters to me now?" resonated deeply. It encouraged me to focus on what holds true value in my life. In essence, "Chaos To Clarity" was more than just a book for me; it was a catalyst, an insightful companion in my personal journey from disorder to understanding.

— Debbie Jenkins
Publishing Consultant and Author

Simon is one my smartest students and became a dear friend who I've known for over twenty years. He has a unique playful quick mind and such a big heart. I view Simon as one of the many blessings in my life. In Tai Chi Chuan the ultimate level is to become a "Supreme Fool" dancing with the Tao, and it was a pleasure to acknowledge and give Simon that title. He is brilliant!

— Katherine Allen
Award Winning Author Teacher Tai Chi Chuan

I've known Simon for a number of years, he is an incredibly creative individual. I like the vision he has and the ideas he creates. I think he is one of the most creative and intelligent persons I've ever met. A true business expert who can help entrepreneurs and business owners tremendously. I thoroughly recommend Simon as a person to work with and consult with.

— **Ernesto Verdugo**
Author, Speaker, Change Catalyst

Simon is the most multi-faceted, extraordinary neural network I've ever come across. A true genius and I'm proud to call him my friend.

— **Michael Trigg**
The Presentation Maestro

Chaos to Clarity is a transformational read that is essential for anyone wanting to make practical change and take hold of their life to move forward with intentionality and focus. These distinctions and working with Simon have been very valuable to me and 100% recommended.

— **Sarah Moxom**
Entrepreneur, Speaker, and Founder Fireside Whispers

I am impressed by your ability to write. Random thinking can lead to clarity of thought which is one of the most important attributes for which to strive.

— **Nigel Roffey**

Simon writes with the enthusiasm of a student and the experience of an old soul. Unwinding our inner desires and frustrations seems an impossible task, but Simon effortlessly provides the tools to untangle these aspects of our lives with poise and wit. A must for all those in need of a mental reset.

—**James Ed**
Founder Be Heard

Anytime I talk with Simon, I always value his unique perspectives and clear passion for adding value to people. I run more than five huge product launches each year and there is always chaos to navigate. I love the way his book naturally has the reader consider new powerful perspectives.

Definitely recommended – Simon's Chaos To Clarity is a must read!

— Matt McWilliams
Bestselling Author of Turn Your Passions Into Profits

In Chaos to Clarity, Simon has masterfully crafted a literary work that resonates deeply with my personal appreciation of the value, importance, and relevance of time.

Drawing on my own military experience, I saw time and again how chaos occurs and how it was vital for real leaders to have and share clarity. This transformative guide offers practical distinctions that empower individuals to reclaim their sanity in a chaotic world and be better able to produce real results in business or indeed on the battlefield.

The insightful anecdotes and step-by-step approach build elegantly and provide a compelling roadmap for anyone looking to truly lead their lives especially in the ever-changing world of today. The thought provoking questions in each chapter empower readers to embark on a journey of self-discovery.

This book is a powerful tool for anyone seeking profound personal growth and meaningful transformation, and I recommend it 100%.

— Brigadier Sushil Bhasin
Military Inspired Leadership Expert,
Global Keynote and TEDx Speaker, Author

Chaos to Clarity provides you with a roadmap to help better understand what really matters in life. This book is for the seeker who wants to understand what motivates them to do what they do and why they do it.

Simon shares stories from his life and others that helped him better understand himself and others. Today self-awareness is the most critical element in a leader's success. We need to have a proven process that allows us to clarify what we know and believe. We need it to help define what really matters to us and the people we care for.

The book shares definitions and exercises that remove fuzziness around the edges of our lives. What if you had the ability to see what is really happening around you? This book provides focus on what's important in our lives. By providing a well thought out multi-disciplinary framework, we can go from Chaos to Clarity in life's most challenging situations.

This book is for the person who wants to explore their motivations, understand what really matters and how to achieve their goals. If you're up for the challenge and willing to do the work, you'll find answers to many questions that have left you wondering is this all there is? It takes you from Chaos to Clarity!

— **Tripp Braden**
Managing Partner Strategic Performance Partners

The Author

Simon is a recognised genius with a unique beautiful mind and capacity to connect the dots in ways that produce predictable profitable results.

For over two decades Simon has been primarily working by referral and often behind the scenes as "**Simon X**". You can think of him as **The Secret Weapon for Good People Doing Great Things.** Some of his clients describe him as a Strategic Alchemist, a master of Ontology, Numbers and Connections and so much more who consistently is able to Make The Difference™.

Having graduated from Durham University with a Mathematics degree, he qualified as a Chartered Accountant with PriceWaterhouseCoopers in the Banking & Capital Markets division in London. While there his focus on what matters uncovered a large multi-billion-pound global fraud. He went on to be head hunted for a decade across a number of major banks where he helped shape new business streams and transform old practices. Specifically, he was responsible for the day-to-day management of over 1 billion in assets under management across multiple European exchanges.

During and since his time in banking he has been involved globally in countless projects and industries, playing a key part in the journeys of many of the well-known names of today. His clients, associates and partners have gone on to generate billions of pounds in revenue, and positively impact millions of people.

In parallel over the decades, he has researched and studied creativity, optimisation, and Human Potential – becoming a master practitioner and trainer of multiple modalities. He applied these learnings competing at elite levels in various sports including Fencing and won triple Golds in the 1996 British Tai Chi

Chuan Open, as well as training and working with countless elite performers from sports to business through to special projects.

He is a sought-after advisor, consultant and speaker and loves to work tactically and strategically with forward facing founders and authorities to help them optimally scale their ideas and impact.

Contents

When you know what really matters, you improve your ability to cut through the noise and give yourself the choice to navigate your life successfully no matter the Chaos and circumstances you find yourself and the world in.

If this is true, and you want to navigate life successfully, then The Key Question™ you must explore and keep considering is:

"**Do I know what really matters to me now?**"

Simon Hedley | Strategic Alchemist™

Acknowledgments

This book is not just 'my book'; it is the result of an extraordinary collaboration with countless individuals who have generously supported and influenced its creation.

I am deeply grateful for the magical moments and insightful conversations shared with Anna, April, Andrew, Bill, Chris, Dave, Ernesto, Graham, Jay, Jenn, Joe, Karen, Katherine, Ken, Luke, Michael, Miti, Neslyn, Noah, Paul, Penny, Rachel, Rae, Ramona, Richard, Sarah, Simon and Terry. Each person's unique contributions, be it encouragement, ideas, or expertise, has left an indelible mark on me and this work.

I would love to extend special thanks to Dr Hedley, Dr Hunt, The Family, My Teachers, Mentors, Clients, Associates and Partners. I am humbled by your unwavering support and inspiration. Gratitude also goes to the incredible teams and all those who played a part in making this possible including the members and teams at Author Marketing Group™, We Design Brands™, The Simple Idea™, The Club™ and Freedom International NOW™.

To the readers and audience, your engagement and interest in my work over the years drive me to continually improve and push the boundaries of my ideas. I am excited to embark on this journey together and look forward to the future's possibilities.

Lastly, I must acknowledge the profound impact of numerous authors, speakers, and coaches throughout my life and history. Their wisdom and insights have guided me on this path, shaping not only this book but also my vision for the future. Thank you all for being part of this incredible journey.

acknowledgments

Introduction

It's a privilege and honour to introduce you to Chaos To Clarity™, and I'm genuinely excited for you. I've written this book as I really believe that the concepts and distinctions it covers, which have taken me over four decades to uncover and curate, really are necessary to help people survive this chaotic world and set themselves up to really thrive. It also matters to me to pay it forward, and having had some personal challenges, I didn't want what I've learnt to die with me. I do love working with people one to one and in group settings, but there is no way I can speak and work with everyone I'd love to, and this is where the book comes in. It gives everyone the blueprint and roadmap and principles that I've used to help thousands produce breakthroughs and more. I believe that if you win, we all win. I'm your raving fan, and perhaps you'll become mine too.

The big idea at the heart of the book is that we can all learn how to transform from being with the reality of Chaos into the possibility of Clarity. However, when people don't know how to be and aren't able to actually be with the reality of Chaos, they're doomed to be delayed and destroyed by it. As we gain increased Clarity, we can access a whole different experience of life and a quantum shift in our ability to produce and enjoy real results in business and the world.

The subtitle of this book is "How to get out of your own way and remember what really matters", and I want to start with being clear that when I say, "what really matters", I'm not going to lecture you on my philosophy or force feed set views on what should matter to you and the world. Far from it: this is about you and what matters to you. I wrote this book for you. My primary focus is to add value to you and your life.

So, this is about what really matters to you. Not just theory and pleasantries, but what truly matters to you. Reading this book is designed to make a difference to you and help you get really clear on what matters to you now and into the future – some of which you may know and some of which you may never have realised, and may even truly surprise you.

I'm also talking about a Clarity about what matters this moment, this hour, this day, this week, this month, this year, this decade, this lifetime and beyond. Few of us have this down – fully consciously understood and mastered – and I've come to believe it's a journey not a destination. We also get to decide and choose – especially what really doesn't matter for us.

While you don't have this Clarity, the likelihood is you're going to be wasting opportunities and resources, and potentially growing, moving, and building towards a destination that's moving you further away from what you really want. Worse, you may not even realise, and in the extreme not realise until it's too late.

It's not about philosophical theory or "magical concepts"; this is about real grounded nuts and bolts and mechanics of the world we live in and are a part of.

More than that, it will give you insights and tools so that you can more effectively create and experience more of what matters to you to experience in your reality. At the same time, it will help you avoid and navigate the noise and confusion that's dragging down people all over the world, and leading many to increasing levels of frustration, despair, regret, and worse.

To reiterate, this book is about producing real results for you. By reading it you will experience more Clarity and know with increasing certainty what really matters to you, and how to navigate your world.

I've learnt not to make assumptions and to zero our expectations, so I want to be clearer who this book is for. It's for people who are committed to playing an active role in producing results in their life – personal, business, and legacy. This book is for you if you're willing to be real and courageous with yourself and learn some challenging information that can give you an access to reality in ways that many will never have.

If you're an entrepreneur or in business, then this book will be very valuable to you, and you'll be able to apply the principles and approaches to your business planning and growth. These ideas have been forged in the real world of business and banking.

If you're a professional or help others produce results, I know you'll love this book, and it will give you greater insights and distinctions so you can make more difference to others. The ideas in these pages have helped me help my clients have extraordinary lives and results, and they will do this for you too.

If you're curious about the world and a "lifelong learner", then I know the book will give you increased creativity and insights into a world that will unlock the extraordinary realms of what's possible in new ways.

As I write this book, I'm living in times and in a world that is massively dynamic and changing. The intensity and ferocity of these changes is building and accelerating. For most this isn't just life and business as usual, but a sign of something they feel and sense (and even know) they aren't prepared optimally for, if at all.

I want to add that thanks to my clients, friends, and mentors – and "luck" – I have been privileged over the decades to have access to a lot of confidential information, technology, and data. Much of this isn't public yet, and the ramifications are truly profound. This book will help you surf the waves that are coming. Change is inevitable, they say; do you agree?

I'm sure you've noticed how more and more people have been thrown into the more extreme aspects of the dance of life by recent changes, developments, and Chaos. We've all been through moments in the last few years when we've said or heard someone say, "I never would have believed this could happen" and "I really don't know what to do."

For some, it's been devastating to realise that the paradigms they lived inside and the people they believed had integrity, had their needs and interests at heart, and were their "wise elders" are being shown to not have been who they thought all along.

For others, we're watching more and more of the people we love and care about show up in burnout, breakdown, and with seemingly fewer and fewer resources to turn things around. Email, mobile, and electronic communications, and the very social media that we thought were going to bring us together, have in fact become some of our greatest challenges to navigate – in reality filling us with disinformation, marketing spin, and fake views of what is real for others and possible for us.

Due to this a lot of people are asking different questions, having to reset, and wondering how to navigate this radically different world optimally. They are also wondering where to focus and how to live a life that few have planned for, let alone predicted.

At the same time some of these challenges have been with us from the beginning and are perhaps part of the nature of what it is to be human. We do however have a chance to explore our unique perspective and perhaps take a different approach now.

For now, in this introduction, we can define:

Chaos as a state of complete disorder and confusion.

Clarity as coherent, understandable, and definite.

These are oversimplifications. Yet we must start somewhere.

So, what happens when humans are in Chaos?

When we are in Chaos, we experience more:

BREAKDOWNS:

There are breakdowns – communications, relationships, systems, technologies – and as a result things take more time, energy, and money to finish, if they can be at all.

NEGATIVES:

There is dissatisfaction – internally and externally. This can be visible or hidden.

EMPTINESS:

There is a lack of energy, resources, or people – internally or externally.

WASTE:

There is often a lack of momentum or optimisation, and as a result, waste.

Instead, if we could be in Clarity, we can usually experience more:

INTEGRITY:

With people and systems, we experience more reliable consistent expected results and there is greater ongoing workability.

POSITIVES:

There is satisfaction – internally and externally there is recognition and reward.

FULLNESS:

There is often a flow and momentum and abundance of energy, resources, opportunities, and people – internally or externally.

EFFICIENCIES:

Things are streamlined and orchestrated, and resources seem to be available as they are needed, with little wastage.

It's worth noting for now that often people's perceptions of reality are off. This is because sometimes – in fact often – our own way of measuring is not as clear as we'd like. Especially when we're in Chaos.

In fact, I've found – and perhaps you've had this experience – that years later, with hindsight, we realise that we had in essence seen "up" as "down", or missed what for others was obvious all along.

So, given these options, "Chaos" or "Clarity", almost everyone would say they would choose to be in Clarity; however is that really the priority?

Will people do whatever it takes to get to and stay in Clarity? Is that even possible?

Will you?

So this book will help show you what's possible and give you the principles to make the possibility of Clarity and all its benefits your reality.

I also want you to consider this question, "Can someone even make that choice authentically when they are in a state of Chaos?"

I really don't think they can, so being real and just for you – right now what is your priority?

Yourself, your business, or something else?

The truth is that Prioritisation is one of the keys to moving from Chaos To Clarity™, and no matter how large the undertaking, it always begins with a first step. This is one of the subjects I go into in the book. It's also a subject that I've found is massively misunderstood and used incorrectly.

For now, know that if we're not clear what really matters, there really is no way to prioritise effectively.

It is also important to note that seemingly distinct aspects and areas of life do interact more than we realise, especially in today's hyper-connected world.

The world is dynamic and holistic, and this is part of the challenge. Our minds cannot handle all the information at one time, and even if they could we can't get access to it in a linear fashion. Could you imagine reading every page on Wikipedia? Or watching every YouTube video?

So now, for all our good intentions, we have a world that is more than ever likely to lead us to the point of system Chaos.

As you read and explore this book, you'll see more and more what's possible and the benefits for you. Some will be clear linear benefits, and some for now may be invisible and unpredictable for you – yet they *are* predictable, as you'll see.

You are also going to have insights, and if you'll take note of them and be with the process, I know this book can be a great asset for you.

Hopefully this introduction has you intrigued and excited to explore the reality of Chaos and the possibility of Clarity. It's been an adventure creating this book, and I hope it serves you.

I wanted to acknowledge you for investing in yourself to read this and thank you. Truly thank you.

So, let us begin to powerfully explore the reality of Chaos, and from there a whole new world of possibilities and a new way to harness it, so that you can move forward towards what really matters for you.

Chapter 1

The Reality of Chaos

"In the midst of chaos, there is also opportunity."

— Sun Tzu

I promised that this book would create real results for you, and so we must begin with the reality of Chaos.

We're going to get present to what Chaos is and why Chaos exists and, in the process, consider how we as a species tend to be with Chaos, and more importantly how you currently relate to it.

We'll explore how errors in understanding the reality of Chaos limit our thinking and results production, and what becomes possible as we get present to the reality of Chaos.

Chaos is a state of complete disorder and confusion. Events and actions occur unpredictably and without any recognisable pattern.

Chaos can arise in many different contexts, including in the physical world (such as chaotic weather patterns), in social systems (such as political upheavals or riots), or even in the individual psyche (such as in cases of mental illness or emotional turmoil).

Chaos can be both destructive and creative, as it can lead to the breakdown of existing structures and the emergence of new ones. It is a complex and dynamic phenomenon that can be difficult to understand or predict by its very nature, and yet it is seemingly an integral foundation of both the natural world and human experience.

Story: If you want to make God laugh, tell her your plans

I host a special annual event called Fresh*Flow*. It runs from exactly 9am to 9pm on the 9th of September. In 2022, with the lockdown finally easing and with my health finally improved, I spent months planning and preparing for the big day on the 9th of September. I had invested heavily in terms of time and money in the venue, technology to showcase, presentation preparation, and professional camera crews to capture the event and create assets for the guests. I also had incredible surprises that even I was blown away by. I was super excited and grateful for the team that had come together to collaborate to make this happen. I had even secured a castle as the venue for the event.

My partners and I had carefully curated the attendees, and everything seemed to be coming together like clockwork, until just a week before the event, when the award-winning photographer cancelled – despite having been contracted months before. She had her reasons: a "job" that seemed better/more important for her had come up that she didn't think she was going to get, and she very unprofessionally bailed on her commitment with just five days' notice and without any real apology, offer of compensation, or intention to help fix the obvious problem.

I called and spoke with the other videographer, and he was shocked at how she'd acted, yet we'd both been around the block, and we came up with a plan. That's one of my fortes – finding solutions – and we were determined to make it work. Then 48 hours before the event he calls and sheepishly says, "Simon, you're not going to believe me or forgive me. I can't make it to the rehearsal tomorrow, and I can't make Friday either; a client just called and they use me regularly and if I don't shoot for them, I might lose them and I'm sorry." I was dumbfounded. Two different companies cancelling in the week just before the event. "I promise I'll find you someone" were his final words. So much for integrity and honouring your agreements.

Creating top quality assets for the attendees was one of the surprises and essential for them to leverage the opportunities I knew we had lined up for those that passed our partner selection on the day. It was also important for me with what I had committed to, and on the back of losing some of my most important mentors and friends to cancer in the last few years, and my own health challenges, I knew that this event would not be able to be repeated.

Yes, I had my own kit and backups and triple redundancies for the kit, but as you can imagine you can't lead an event and take the photos and videos at the same time. So, I scrambled to find a replacement at a higher cost, but still felt confident that the event would be a success.

The day before the event, I was flat out busy preparing the venue and transporting everything across. The weather was great, and I was excited for what was sure to be an amazing event. Then as we went to set up the banner displays, the base of the display turned out to be defective. Stressful phone calls later and a save from one of my secret weapons, and we were all set as I drove back 30 minutes at 5pm for the VIP dinner.

So, there I was, at the dinner, as the VIPs started to arrive – some of whom I had never met in person and who had travelled from different parts of the UK, and even flown in from the United States and Ibiza. Everyone was laughing and having a great time, when suddenly my phone rang.

It was the senior director of the venue, and they had some devastating news to share – the Queen had died, and they were closing the venue for at least seven days. They needed all our event materials and technology removed before 7am for a special remembrance event, and to make an already stressful mission impossible, neither I nor anyone else could get into the venue before 6:30am.

I was completely floored. Not only were they talking about moving hundreds of thousands of pounds of equipment that had taken a day to setup in 30 minutes. They had no suggestions or solution for a backup event.

More than that, the passing of the Queen had major ramifications and was a huge loss to many of the people I know who had worked with and for her over decades. The game had changed in that instant in ways that almost none of the general public could ever imagine, and most will never know.

What happened next – how we managed to attend the remembrance event that morning at 7am as a group, get everything moved, and run the event in a whole different way, and all the ramifications of that phone call – which are still going on today – well for brevity we'll save that for another day.

How would you have felt when the VIP guests asked, "Everything ok?" at the dinner just after the phone call?

I walked outside and had to take a few moments to Pause Stop Reset – or at least try to. I started thinking, then making phone calls, and as I walked back inside, I put a smile on my face and tried to remember what really matters.

As I'm sharing this now, it points to what I've learnt experientially and will be sharing with you more in this book. I'm sure you've had moments like this in your life, and I've had countless others I could share. What's important is that you start to think about how much can and does go wrong, or is unpredicted, that points at the wider Chaos that's there pushing to take over our plans.

I do want to acknowledge and share a huge thanks to my Queen, and to my mum – who let me pull a "rabbit out of the hat" and was fortunate to have met Her Majesty on several occasions – and to all those who navigated the Chaos and made things work so that, like our VIP guests, many people just woke up thinking the world was "normal".

One of those people is a man who I've been lucky to call a real friend for over twenty years. He made the difference to me and the family that day. His experience and training with emergencies and special forces gives him a different mindset to others. If you want to get an idea of his dry humour, when we spoke after we finally stowed away all the kit on the 10th, he said, "Well the lesson is, you needed to plan better; after all, why didn't you have *not just one but at least two* backup venues?"

The bigger irony: virtually all the footage we did manage to get, that we ended up paying over the odds for, is unusable. Most importantly though, those VIP guests who attended still received the promise of the event and many have had incredible breakthroughs since.

As I write this I'm smiling, as in many ways it's the perfect exemplary story, and I can see how my painful, expensive experience can service this moment now and this book and you. Which is what matters to me right now.

P.S.

One of my friends read this story and said I wrote it in a way that seemed angry. Am I angry at the photographer and videographer? Not really, that wouldn't help anything. Disappointed in what happened and how they communicated afterwards, 100%. More groundedly, I was angry at myself more than anything and frustrated that "Chaos" won the day yet again.

Beating myself up for not doing better is not a habit I wish on anyone else, yet one that I know I have a tendency to fall back into. Now many months later I'm still left with a bitter taste in my mouth – regret – as it could have been avoided, and the ripples of what didn't happen and what did continue.

Unexpected Chaos often prompts people to react with frustration and anger – even if those very emotions do very little to help apart from potentially causing more Chaos. When we experience a primary emotion like fear, loss, or sadness, this emotion creates feelings of vulnerability and loss of control which are uncomfortable. One way of attempting to deal with these feelings is by subconsciously shifting into anger.

One way to start to unpack and transform "the anger" is to consider:

- What did I expect that didn't happen?
- What did I intend to happen that was stopped?
- What was not communicated?

In this Fresh*Flow* story, I expected, having hired and paid professionals, to get great shots or at least workable ones. I intended to use the shots and footage to create value for the guests and promote future events and for legacy value. There was no real apology communicated or responsibility accepted, and I've held back from really sharing how much I didn't get what I paid for and really thought about them.

Insights / Distinctions:

Are you ready for some good and bad news?

We exist and we don't really know how.

We live somewhere that isn't fully in our control. We are impacted by weather, other people, and so many things we aren't even aware of.

As I write this, and for most of the readers I expect to read this in the near term, we live somewhere on a planet called Earth. This planet we haven't really explored fully, and even what we have explored most of us don't have awareness of let alone a real experience of.

Our planet is unstable and dynamic with moving tectonic plates, atmospheres, and oceans which are in a state of motion and change. It manifests as not always "human friendly" and reveals its unstable nature in the form of earthquakes, floods, volcanic eruptions, droughts, landslides, lightning, hurricanes, tsunamis and more.

We live in a reality of Chaos that is so chaotic that we do all we can to pretend we have a semblance of control. When in reality we have none, not in the great scheme of things.

Mathematics will tell you about probabilities, but in the extreme the past does not predict the future.

In recent times, Chaos and its impact on our world and our lives has come knocking. We must have empathy for others and ourselves – and there are so many people globally going through a world that is more and more challenging.

There have been extremely difficult times before – global pandemics, world wars, food shortages, "evil" dictatorships, and worse.

It's likely there will be again.

On a personal level, we don't know what to expect – not only do we not know what's possible; it's also becoming harder to know what's "groundedly" probable. After all, if I'd said it would be illegal to meet up with your own family here in the UK a few years ago, I'd have been laughed at as "crazy". Yet, during the lockdown, that was the case.

We see so much in the "news media" that we've come to know we can't trust and often isn't the whole story – either by chance or deliberately altered. Most people are somewhat smarter to the fact that there are giant lobbying companies, and conflicts of interest, between an "unbiased media" and the needs for sponsorship by advertisers.

Institutions that we've thought would be there forever have come and gone, and many that were some of the largest in the world vanished overnight. Some of the legendary founders and leading entrepreneurs have been discovered to be worse than frauds.

Has this always been this case? Are we just getting smarter or more informed? Or is there something else we're starting to notice?

I'm sure most people know someone who has gone through a bad relationship breakdown, or had a major health challenge, or lost their job suddenly, or had a major investment loss. In some ways these are all parts of "life" and the modern world. Yet the very nature of our lives and expectations and the institutions we make our lives around has transformed over the last few centuries. We've shifted from a world that was linked to nature and the land to one that is so abstracted that many people do work that has no correlation to or transparency with the food they rely on daily to survive.

If we're not present to the seasons and cycles of life, and that reality of growing and harvesting food, how can we really be connected to the world we live in?

I spent over a decade in "The City" of London, often being at my desk before dawn and leaving after dusk. There were days when I didn't go outside all day. This wasn't ideal, and looking back now with the distinctions I have, I don't know how I and so many others just got on with it day after day (and others still do).

When I was at Durham University, studying mathematics, one of the areas I focussed on was Dynamic Systems. The example that most stands out in my mind today is that of the unicycle. Have you ever tried to ride one? There is a similarity with a bicycle, and it's also a whole different skillset and experience.

The unicycle is almost constantly in motion and in a state of falling over. That's actually the key to its stability and to being able to ride one.

The physics at play with gravity and momentum want the unicycle to fall to the ground. If you imagine a unicycle that could be balanced perfectly upright, the slightest breeze or nudge in any direction and over it would go. Eventually it would crash to the ground and then stay still – this ground state being seemingly stable.

So, we have the unicycle seemingly stable but with the slightest input heading to stable ground. This is a good reference frame for how most of modern life is. We have built structures and systems and even ecosystems that without much nudging want to crash and fall to zero. Yet there is seeming stability. How can this be so?

Well like the unicycle, we can individually and collectively keep taking steps to move us back towards what we feel is stable.

Governments do this when they vary their interest rates and fiscal policies.

Businesses do this when they hire and fire and try new products and marketing approaches.

Yet the reality I want you to see is that with the best will in the world, and even with the biggest commitment of energy and focus and resources, most if not all of this will want to tend to Chaos and eventually succumb back to ground zero.

Even and especially the physical constructions we've generated need ongoing repair. Our solid building materials rust, weather, and corrode – often leaving structures unsafe and in need of giant investments to save them.

Here in the UK, and around the world, coastal erosion is wiping away coastlines, and homes are falling into the sea.

What can we do in the face of Chaos? I would suggest that it encourages us to learn to use our intelligence and get better at what I defined as "Pi Thinking". This is thinking that is unlimited and allows our brain to come up with creative ideas – some perhaps beautiful; others more surreal. Ideas partly based on the past and drawing on all the resources we have consumed and imagined. It's called Pi Thinking after the irrational number π. Pi has an infinite number of digits, so we'll never figure out its exact value no matter how close we seem to get. So it seems to be with the infinite possibilities and ideas that are out there.

It seems obvious in a chaotic world that there is value in being able to be creative and divergent in our thinking – learning to be agile with the random changes of life. Yet this is something that most of us are not good at doing. We like simplicity and all too often get blindsided by Chaos – even and especially of our own making.

Have you ever had a train been delayed and spoil your plans?

Has the weather changed suddenly leaving you unprepared to say the least?

Most people have extremely limited thinking. They haven't learnt to activate their innate ability for Pi Thinking, let alone to optimally leverage it. Chaotic ideas aren't necessarily helpful if they aren't able to be channelled, filtered, and dialled in.

Pi Thinking allows us to tap back into the truly infinite nature of possibilities. When we do, we can see steps we can take inside the Chaos that may move us forward, and we can choose to take them. Most never even imagine these steps are there to take, so don't.

After all, you can't ask where the lift is, or press the button and wait for one, if you don't know one exists. At least if you can imagine there might be one, you can choose to explore how to take it.

When you wake up in the morning, billions of people have been acting on ideas overnight. Some of those actions change everything in an instant, and others, seemingly insignificant, cause us to reach and go past tipping points, like the last snowflake landing causing a branch to break.

There are new lives entering our world, and many who have passed – often without any warning.

Yet we want to believe the world hasn't changed. As humans we want things to stay the same – or at least we've learnt to want that in order to find some comfort in the Chaos, to believe we're ok and will survive.

Even as you read this sentence, the world is changing and transforming.

For many, this Chaos leads to one emotion underlying everything – fear. Our ancestors knew it as they tried to find solace in the dark, as they hunted for nutrients and shelter, as so many things they didn't understood shook their world.

Are we really that far removed when we scrape back the trappings of "civilisation"?

Thought Experiment:

To get a sense of Chaos and how you relate to it, try on this thought experiment.

I want you to imagine you wake up tomorrow, and you're in a superfast vehicle that can travel in any direction for any time without needing to stop or refuel.

You would really like to get back home (or another destination of your choosing).

However, you can't see where you are, you can't see where you're going, and you have no idea which was is up or north, or the direction your home is in.

Also, around you and the vehicle, the land keeps moving – turning and twisting – and you can't even tell by how much or when it will happen.

What would you do?

Would you ever get home?

How does this thought experiment feel so far?

If you'd like the extras for experts, try on that you also don't know how to pilot or control the vehicle, and you woke up in it but without anyone letting you know what we shared above.

This old quote comes to mind, "Out of the frying pan, hopefully not into the fire."

The Key Questions:

- Could I predict the weather four hundred years from now with absolute accuracy and certainty? What about a year from now?
- What do I keep wishing I could control but have no control over?
- Has something I never expected to happen completely stopped my plans in their tracks?

Summary:

In this chapter we explored the reality of Chaos, and how it's the very nature of the world and reality we live inside of.

The media are going to constantly highlight more and more "bad news" as it gets eyeballs and in turn sponsors and advertisers. We are in a time of change, most of which is predictably unpredictable, and that's unlikely to change anytime soon (but even that could). Most people globally feel powerless and don't have a real clear plan on how to move forward; they're just present to the fact that things aren't working.

We've seen huge billion-pound banks and businesses file for bankruptcy, global mega-frauds and Ponzi schemes, and there is no safe system or bet about "who we can trust".

We've seen health challenges come out of left field and the world as we knew it thrown out of the window with no notice or ability to affect change – especially with the enforced no-fly zones and lockdowns.

We've started to pull back the curtains we use to hide the true Chaos that surrounds and makes up the world we live in.

Now we have the start of a foundation we can build on – and remember that the first step in transformation is often seemingly "bad/confronting news".

Chapter 2

The Possibility of Clarity

"Truth is ever to be found in simplicity, and not in the multiplicity and confusion of things."

— Isaac Newton

As we highlighted in the first chapter on The Reality of Chaos, almost everyone has at one point or another felt like they are drowning in a sea of Chaos and confusion. It's all too common when I'm talking to friends or clients for them to share that they feel like they are constantly juggling too many things at once and can't seem to see the light ahead of this ever changing scenario. I know they're not alone; after all, in today's fast-paced world, it's easy to become overwhelmed and lost in the noise.

What if I told you that there's a way out of the Chaos? A way to cut through the clutter and find Clarity in your thoughts and actions? It may seem like an impossible dream, but the truth is that Clarity is within reach for all of us.

In this chapter, we'll explore the possibility of Clarity and the transformative power it can have in your life and business. We'll start to examine the practical steps you can take to gain Clarity in your own life, and why this must start with being open to the possibility of Clarity.

So, take a deep breath, smile if you can, and just for now put aside what usually keeps your mind busy and hooked, and join me on a journey to discover the possibility and power of Clarity. If all goes to plan, then together we'll unlock even more of the potential that lies within each of us and find a perhaps surprising path forward towards a more fulfilling and meaningful life.

Story:

He was seething with anger, his eyes narrowed in determination. His breath pushed heavily through his nose as we faced each other on the mat, just outside of arms' reach. I knew this was going to be a fight to remember. He lunged forward, grabbing at me with all his might, and with his whole focus being to beat me at all costs.

It was the final match of the British Tai Chi Chuan Open in 1996. I found myself facing an opponent I had already beaten twice earlier that day. This time I had been asked to compete at a weight category higher than my own – a good test for me, Dan (Dan Docherty, the father of practical tai chi chuan in the West) had told Katherine (my teacher).

The second time I had faced him was a surprise, and now this was beyond a joke, I thought. Each time I faced him his anger and frustration had notched up. He was older than me, and this was my first time competing. I didn't know what to expect.

The energy of this competition and the raised fighting areas was a far cry from the school sports and county matches I was used to in Fencing or Judo.

The first time we shook hands, the second time barely, and this time all sportsmanship had gone from his face.

The crowd was buzzing with anticipation, and the noise kept building, but as the referee signalled the start of the match, everything around me faded away. I was focused on one thing and one thing only. It might surprise you, but it wasn't winning. I was present in the moment, feeling the ground beneath my feet and the breath flow in and through me.

My opponent was relentless, attacking with a ferocity I had never seen before or since. He was like a man possessed compared to before.

There wasn't time for me to do an analysis or come up with a plan. Years of training and decades of movie watching boiled down to the Clarity and reality of this moment. For the next few minutes, I had one thing to focus on. He was there in front of me and intending to do me harm. I was clear I wasn't moving outside of the ring. I was the mountain. I was the air. I was, and beyond that there was no me. Just awareness. No separation.

All his energy and pushing didn't drive and damage the way he planned. Instead, it simply revealed his "void" (the area of no resistance) to me with such a blazing Clarity that it almost compelled my body to push into it. I swayed back with his attack and simultaneously spiralled around as my legs, arms, and weight connected and sprung forward and out.

In that moment something magical happened: all of me – my mind, body, spirit – moved as one, and without any forcing I flowed like the mother tiger coming down the mountain side to protect her cubs. Yet still I was rooted like seaweed to the granite rock during the wildest storms. Everything was getting more intense and building in the silence and stillness.

Then there he was sailing out of the ring, and I watched curious as to why or how – my opponent's more than twelve stones flying through the air like a pillow, in a way that I couldn't have repeated if you'd offered to pay me a million pounds.

I had in that moment moved as we had trained a thousand times. I could say I effortlessly rooted myself and diverted his attack masterfully. That would be a lie. I don't know what happened in that moment. I didn't have a million thoughts to contend with. There was no trying to be clever or funny.

This experience was distinctly different, and something I had never experienced before in practice – perhaps because in practice the opponents (my friends) had never been focussed on my destruction at all costs.

The audience jumped from their seats, cheering and shouting as the judge moved to raise my hand in victory. In that moment out of time and space, there was no I trying to do anything or needing anything. I wasn't tired. Far from it, it was as if a light switch had been flipped on.

As I looked at Katherine – my dear beloved friend and true teacher no longer with us, Katherine Allen – she smiled and gave me a nod.

Breath flowed back into me, and my body started to move; I was at peace.

"Simon, I don't know how you did that. You won."

Insights / Distinctions:

Out of all the infinite possibilities, you can make choices and decisions. The word decision means to cut off and away when we look at its original Latin roots. When we cut away the Chaos, what are we left with?

What we choose.

We get to say left or right when we get to the fork in the road.

In a single moment, you can get Clarity on your next step, especially once you've made decisions and committed to them.

Once we set our goal – our target – then we can get laser focussed.

Psi Thinking is how we describe this absolute laser-focussed harnessing of our intelligence towards reaching our goal. Why is it called Psi Thinking? Perhaps after the Greek symbol Ψ. Perhaps a nod to the measure of pressure – pound-force per square inch.

Imagine the hawk high in the sky, locking onto its moving target, waiting until the moment is right – and then all is committed.

The peregrine falcon is diving at incredible speeds of more than 300 km /186 miles per hour – all the while navigating with intelligence the air currents and movements needed to achieve its end.

So we can be that way, and in fact the most successful people get good at doing this. They get hooked onto an idea and then do whatever it takes to make it a reality.

Have you had one of these experiences?

Distractions clearly are a challenge, and yet how do we know what's a distraction, what is an aid towards our goal, a short cut, or something else. How do we have time for these thoughts in these moments? Time is part of the key to this that we'll come back to later in the book. For now, let's keep it simple – we're focussed on the possibility of Clarity, and inside that context, anything that doesn't help us communicate and share what's necessary is a distraction.

What is possible is to keep going moment by moment towards your goal. Yes, you can use Pause Stop Reset™ to help you navigate and all the while be there fully present looking for what's next.

I like to imagine a dolphin dancing as the waves break ahead of the shore. There is absolute Clarity in the moment, it seems. No worry about job titles for the dolphin. It's not looking for food or fighting off a shark. In the moment as it leaps and spins, it's there.

Of course, we can't know the mind of a dolphin – and perhaps not even another human, not fully – yet we can learn to know our own mind.

We can build our certainty as to what we are not and what we say is not for us and is a distraction. I suggest starting with the negative as that's sometimes easier for us to carve away.

We can learn to have confidence in our competence and capacity in the moment, and our focus.

We can know from grounded, hard-won experience that come what may, we can handle ourselves and function – or at least that we'll do our best in each moment when we remember.

What if these moments, like pearls, could be threaded together, moving from one space of Clarity to another.

Thought Experiment:

Let's imagine for a second that you had absolute insight and intelligence. You knew with certainty the consequences of your actions and inactions. All the infinite possibilities, probabilities and potentialities were spread out in front of you for your exploration and enquiry. All the while your consciousness and creativity have the capacity to easily handle and process this information.

In that state you would be able to pick and choose the paths and steps you take and the results and experiences you'll receive.

How would you feel in each moment?

Would you ever be "lost" or "conflicted"?

The Key Questions:

- What do I want to experience now?
- What is the one thing I want to complete right now?
- What doesn't matter right now?
- How can I make this happen now?

Summary:

In this chapter we've started to explore the possibility of Clarity.

We've glimpsed at something that is distinct from Chaos, and lives in the moment.

This points at a world that would cause our experience of life and business and the future to be transformed.

We've started the inquiry into Clarity and what really matters, which we'll explore for the rest of this book.

Chapter 3

Learning to Learn

"The capacity to learn is a gift;
the ability to learn is a skill;
the willingness to learn is a choice."

- Brian Herbert

We come into this world as newborns as seemingly almost infinite sponges for knowledge and learning.

Some would argue we come into the world a complete blank, but not me. For myself I think we come in with some pre-existing hardwired skills and capacity and even initial orientations – one of which is the capacity, willingness, and need to learn.

The newborn human, which is apparently helpless, has the ability to connect with warmth and security, to latch onto a breast to gather nutrition, and in time learn to mimic and adapt. This pattern of learning to move, to communicate is seen around the world. Each culture and era has great similarities and also mass variations in this process, and this allows children to communicate with their parents after a few years, even when those same children couldn't necessarily communicate with each other across their newly built language barriers.

For generations, the debate of nature vs. nurture has raged on. In this chapter we're going to explore that a little further with where we, and more specifically you, are today. We'll look and consider how you learnt to learn – carrot/stick, conforming/creating – and more importantly how you could learn to learn optimally now.

I'm going to challenge you now to try on "We don't know how we learn."

From this perspective what opens up? Let's explore…

Story:

As the salty cold ocean water sprayed around me, I kicked to find a space to breathe.

My lungs were working on overdrive to regain balance after I was hurled spinning and tumbling through the air as if by a judo master.

My brain kicked back into gear, recalling from the daze what had happened – the sail had caught a great wind draft pulling it out of my hands, and in the process me forward and out to the right, while the board had lunged down a few metres as the wave crest I was on dropped out.

My eyes darted to see the board now playing hide and seek as the ocean sent it drifting in unknown directions. Then I see it, and in a rapid dozen strokes my hand reaches the strap.

I drag myself onto it with a few sharp efforts, swinging my legs and myself out of the swells and onto its unstable island of calm.

Now I can rest and smile. The sun is beaming, the wild ocean waves around Lanzarote hinting at the ocean's natural power.

Half memories come of still lake waters a decade or so before, struggling to even get onto the board, let alone stand on it.

There were countless falls – hilarious to those watching and frustrating and exhausting to my small young body and brain.

Blistered hands pulled at the rope to try and get the sail an inch out of the water, only to have to give up as my arms gave in, or my lack of balance prevailed.

Now, for the first time in ages I'm out on the water… a stronger, wiser perhaps, me standing on the board, bending down and gently reaching for the mast rope.

Straightening my arm and leaning back, I let the waters flow off the sail and the wind turn the board and sail.

Not fighting, just flow.

Definitely not a master, but a whole different game.

With a flick, the mast and I come up and together. And then adjust back, move hands, and gently we start to move.

Time to head in, or shall we go for a big wave again?

Insights / Distinctions:

So, given our context of "Chaos to Clarity", where do we begin, and I think the best place to do that is with a distinction called "Beginner's Mind". This is a simple idea and also a very advanced mastery level distinction.

It's said to have its origins in Zen Buddhism, where the concept is called *Shoshin* meaning beginner's mind. It refers to having an attitude of openness, eagerness, and lack of preconceptions when studying, even at an advanced level, just as a beginner would.

Trying on "Beginner's Mind" is the idea of viewing things with fresh eyes, as if for the first time, even if you have prior knowledge or experience with the subject.

Have you ever been a beginner at something? Do you remember how you approached the lessons and the teachers? Sadly, as a child often we're told what we have to learn. As we mature, we get freedom to choose what we learn. However, I don't think many of us ever got help as adults learning how to learn optimally.

Just knowing about the idea of beginner's mind does not mean we can master it and apply it during each and every lesson.

I recently, at 44, had my first official guitar lessons, and it was a humbling, confronting, and profound experience to watch myself forced back into beginner's mind and beginner's skills. My years and skills with oboe, piano, DJing, and music production helped and also hindered as my mind tried to unpack and recode what I was being taught. I also had to be with the realisation that to get as good as I would want at playing guitar would likely take years… and potentially never happen. I had to get comfortable with being uncomfortable, and the learning journey and curve. Some would say why choose/decide to learn then? That's a long conversation for another time, but it's safe to say I wouldn't be writing this chapter this way if I hadn't.

I had similar experiences when I went to learn salsa dancing in my early twenties. I was a good athlete growing up and had already competed at national level in fencing and won a gold medal in tai chi, yet those first few beginner salsa lessons had me feeling shocked and ashamed as I stumbled around trying to follow the super confident teachers. All we were doing was stepping to time – left, right, left, right – yet somehow there was no rhythm or control. What made it more fun and workable was other lovely beginners who kept smiling and trying hard. I did progress quickly, and within a month I was up in the improvers class, and then a few months later the advanced class. I'd caught the salsa dancing bug – it was a great way to exercise, meet good people, and escape from my stressful city job as a trainee accountant at PriceWaterhouseCoopers.

What made the difference in going from beginner to advanced? Well partly my stubbornness – I kept going back week after week. My practice in the class and outside of the basic steps. The fact that the teacher at the class I found was a great teacher for beginners helped (and that was by luck more than judgement). Then at a certain point I was able to do some 1:1 intensive lessons very affordably near me with an "old school" traditional dance instructor – an amazing woman who had been teaching dance for maybe forty years.

Finally, the piece which really tipped it over the edge: I went to a Salsa Weekender in, of all places, Butlins in a far away place in the middle of nowhere. Just three days in a place that I never would have otherwise chosen to visit. Yet it was non-stop dancing and lessons, and when I came back, I'd unlocked something – a bit like when you finally crack how to ride a bike – only now I could salsa, and from that foundation I could build. In fact within a year I was teaching beginners salsa for fun and as part of a business I helped grow around "dance dating". What's even more interesting is if my old friend hadn't kept vanishing off dancing, I might never have gone to even one lesson, let alone prioritised it.

Decades later I've had many fun evenings and experiences dancing and helping others learn to dance; seeing them light up as new possibilities reveal themselves and become realities is something that matters to me. I care about people. I think if you're still reading this, perhaps you do to.

Where do we go from here? Well, some of the greatest wisest teachers will tell you that each moment can be your access to priceless lessons and learnings. It's potentially quite confronting to consider that every moment from now on that you are alive is a learning and growing opportunity. I've found more and more, however, that this can be a powerful state to step into.

Also, I can try on and consider how to be a better and better student – when I choose to be – and that's a key distinction. We get to choose when we want to be a student at all, let alone a good one and when we don't. It's very different when you want to learn rather than when you're being told you have to.

After all, you don't want to invest all your time and energy and resources learning things that don't matter and don't help you focus/create/experience more of what matters.

Equally, you don't want to just learn by rote and accept anything and everything that a teacher says. We know and have probably experienced personally how things we thought to be true turned out not to be later.

This chapter is an opportunity for you to consider inside this context of the reality of Chaos and the possibility of Clarity, how you personally (and we collectively) can learn now and into the future.

I think building up your skills and capacity to learn, model, optimise, and master in any domain of knowledge is a priceless skill or process. What do *you* think?

One of the observations of modern science is how much things change. They say each atom in the human body is replaced (depending on the study) every 5–7 years. And 98% of all atoms are replaced after just one year. That's definitely not been my personal experience or observation. So, what do we do with that data? An innocent beginner's mind would accept it as gospel. Perhaps we'd try and validate it and find a published article or some data on the internet. However, hopefully by now you know that just because something is said or published doesn't make it true.

Part of why I'm labouring these points is that part of the path to move from the possibility of Clarity to its probability and experience is a new model for learning and evaluation based on your creativity and consciousness. We're going to shift the access to Clarity from the outer worlds to the inner – and in a grounded way.

Learning itself can be a linear process, but all too often isn't. So, what is it instead?

Learning is a complex and multi-dimensional process that does not follow a linear trajectory to its outcomes. It is unique to each person learning and their intellectual and bio-mechanical specifics. Learning is a dynamic and interactive process that involves cognitive, emotional, social, biological, physical, and even metaphysical factors. It can be influenced by various internal and external factors, including motivation, interest, attention, memory, and environment. To complicate things even more, these may interact in complex ways to influence the quality and effectiveness of the learning experience.

Learning itself is an iterative process that involves trial and error, experimentation, reflection, and refinement. It often involves making mistakes, encountering obstacles, and encountering new information that challenges existing beliefs or knowledge.

Even more fascinating: the risks and rewards, benefits, and gains from learning aren't obvious either. Consider how few children learning to crawl and walk have any real conscious understanding of the rich worlds that they can potentially start to explore. Equally, that choice to learn to say "hello" and "thank you" in a foreign language hides the potential benefits to our personal and business lives in the years to come.

Think about how something that maybe you spent a decade learning and gaining competence in may allow you the opportunity to learn about and leverage something that didn't even exist when you learnt the first thing.

This is especially true in the modern "information" technology age, and I think we'll see more ramifications as we step into a world of advanced AI, avatars, and hyper-connectivity.

As I pointed at before, the "why" to your learning can play a big part in its efficacy and how you are "being" about the learning process.

Now with learning to play guitar, there is a long history – hundreds of years – of established practice and approaches. This is something that I'm guessing millions of humans have managed to learn. Yes, some greats have reached excellence levels that are profound and seem impossible. Consider what the humans of the future may be able to do with different insights and approaches. For me, after a few of the people I cared about inspired my idea to learn, I spoke with one of my clients who is recognised as a master teacher. We'd known each other for years, but it never dawned on me to ask him for a lesson. When I did, the rest was history, as they say, and now, I'm in the process of learning guitar. My sense is that no matter who I was and how much I practised, this would be a lifelong journey. When I shared this with one of my good friends, it turned out he'd been playing for years and used to be in a band or two. His idea of his bad playing – like a beginner, he said – sounded like a professional to me.

Many of the subjects I hold most dear have this quality of being able to learn, explore and master them for lifetimes. That includes learning to be the world's best coach, mentor, and adviser. Learning about myself and my drives and my unique health opportunities and challenges. Learning about how to be there (and be with not being able to be there optimally) with greater empathy and compassion and heart and integrity for the people I care about. More than anything, learning how to make the difference in this moment optimally.

As you read this, perhaps you'll consider what you know you need and want to learn, and how you'll approach those things that show up on your journey.

Will you reach out and find a teacher? A coach? An online course? A workshop? A mastermind? A book? Study buddies?

Assuming you have Clarity on what you want and need to learn, one inquiry will be as to how you choose and prioritise your investment – and I'd encourage you to consider it an investment – of time, energy, money, focus, and other resources.

How will you motivate yourself and navigate the learning dip/wall when all you're doing makes seemingly no progress or difference?

One key I've found is **Pause Stop Reset ™**.

Some of the sagest advice I've been given when I'm hitting the wall while studying is to take a **pause**, congratulate yourself on having taken some action and given it a go – then sleep on it and come back to it another day.

I also want to highlight the distinctions of **The Merlin Method**, where we look back from a future and see what had to happen and who we had to be in order to achieve those outcomes. This can help us learn what we need to learn, and the sequencing of these learnings.

The idea behind this method is to focus on the outcome you want to achieve and then determine the necessary steps or actions required to reach that outcome. It can help provide Clarity and direction by breaking down a larger goal into smaller, manageable tasks. The Merlin Method as I was taught it and teach it is much more nuanced, but for now the general concept of starting with the end in mind and working backwards is a valuable approach for planning and problem-solving, and one I encourage you to add to your toolbox, especially in relation to learning to learn.

Usually, we try and learn forward from where we are – considering what we already know in this moment. When we use The Merlin Method, this shifts to stepping into a future where things have already happened and looking back at what we had to learn and how we made it so. Both approaches are creative and imaginative. The genius in The Merlin Method is that we work back from the outcomes, and in so doing we give ourselves greater Clarity on the path to take and also highlight the potential gaps and challenges that need to be focussed on to succeed. We'll come back to these ideas throughout the book.

Are you familiar with these ideas? How often do you use them? Are you using them optimally? Do you think others do? How could you apply what you're learning already in this chapter?

As you learn – and especially as you look at how to optimally learn to learn for you now – which I do believe will change over time and situationally, the power of asking better questions will become more and more clear.

Questions do something quite profound. In fact, some people say we live inside questions – both conscious to us and underneath our waking minds – that drive all our actions and habits. Perhaps "How can I be safe?" or "How can I be loved?".

Throughout the book I'll share some key questions, and you can add your own here in the book (yes, I really do encourage you to write in the book) and in your journal. (If you're looking for a great journal, I recommend the one I created for myself and my clients which is designed to be flexible in how you use it; you can get your copy here at www.PauseStopReset.com/journal.)

Questions really are powerful, and I could write a whole book on the power and impact of the question. For now, I just want to highlight the gentle danger of asking the wrong questions. They can direct your and others' attention and focus down alleyways with no positive outcomes. You can easily get into a never-ending spin of question following question with no useful traction. The classic movie trope of kids asking, "Are we there yet?" or "Why? Why? Why? Why?" perhaps will serve as a useful reminder.

For now, just start to notice the results of the questions you and others ask, and in time you'll find your own distinctions.

One of my mentors once asked me if I knew The Five W's, and it turned out I did, but not labelled as that. They are five simple one-word questions that can definitely help you move from Chaos To Clarity™.

Do you know The Five W's?

1.
2.
3.
4.
5.

Can you see how I'm giving you a structure to fill in the blanks?

In life we get to give ourselves structures to build our learning onto. Most people haven't learnt to give themselves the foundations and building blocks to learn optimally.

One of these keys is triplification. This is the art of covering something three times, or in three ways, or from three perspectives. Can you see what I did there? Does that make sense? When could you apply triplification?

So, The Five W's – have you worked them out yet? Are you 100% sure? Would you bet everything you have on your answers being correct?

Often, I'd start sharing about this and see if people could complete them. What's interesting I think is that even after they told me with certainty and apparent Clarity that they didn't know them at all – once I started sharing, suddenly they would jump into the conversation saying they did all along.

1. Who?
2. What?
3. When?
4. Where?
5. …

What's the fifth W?

I've done this real-world experiment in training thousands of times to tens of thousands of people over the decades.

Would it surprise you that a percentage couldn't work out the fifth?

What if I told you that over 20% would tell me it was "how"?

I was always surprised by that.

As I learnt it, The fifth W is Why.

Did you predict that?

What did you learn from going through this seemingly unexpected inquiry into The Five W's? Do you see how I used triplification?

So, The Five W's are:

1. Who?
2. What?
3. When?
4. Where?
5. Why?

Now the question is how you can apply The Five W's. I could tell you, but it's going to be more powerful if you start to learn how to use them yourself and actually apply them. Learn to experiment and optimise for yourself.

One way to use them is consider in relation to each goal and focus you have, what the answers are. You may discover that you don't know the answer, or you have a generalised answer like "anyone" or "everyone". This can be useful to point to the fact you don't have the Clarity you may have thought.

In business, often it's very useful to consider who the product, service, event, or experience is for. This ideal client is called a Customer Avatar. Yet as a consultant or coach or in my "strategic alchemy" role, people will often say "everyone". They don't really mean that in a thought-through way. When people get greater Clarity about who their Customer Avatar could be and is, it can have profound benefits, many of which they didn't predict.

Would you like access to my Growth Mechanics™ course on what Customer Avatars are? What if it cost £1,000? How about if I give you access as a gift? Would that be better? Would you use it?

Let's see…

Here's how you can access the course:

1. Go to www.CustomerAvatars.com
2. Use the coupon code CLARITYX, and you'll be able to access the entire course online at no cost.

P.S.

As I write and publish this, I really do intend for you to have the chance to access this course as a gift for having read this far in the book. I've been paid thousands of pounds for this course in the past, and it's helped my clients build many successful businesses. More importantly, this course has helped them help a lot of people move from Chaos into greater and great Clarity in their business and in turn in their lives.

The link and code is designed to be live for a long time; however, I can't be sure when you're reading these words, and I can't promise the offer and coupon code will work forever – I'm aware, and want you to be, that I am providing it on a best-efforts basis.

Consider – after all is there any realistic way that I could guarantee the site and system would still be live a thousand years from now? Think about this as you read the chapter on expectations and intentions later in the book.

Again, in the context of learning to learn, one of my clients sent me this message on WhatsApp last week:

> "Never thought working on my customer avatar could be so interesting or useful.
>
> Always thought of it as a little redundant and time consuming without the payoff.
>
> Think I'm starting to understand what this is about.
>
> Great course.
> Thank you."

What's interesting is, he'd been offered access to the course nearly nine months earlier when we first started working together. He had chosen not to leverage the opportunity it was. Why? Because he thought he knew what there was to learn. It's only now when he had a real need to learn something new, and when he realised that, as he said, he was "stuck", that he allowed me to step in and teach and train and share some insights that he was hungry to learn and apply. Now, less than a week later, he's in momentum and moving towards his goal to help people and earn what will be a breakthrough income for him.

What changed was that his desire to learn increased massively. He also had got to the point where he was willing to learn in different ways and took my suggestion even though he didn't know where it would go. I'd earnt the right to teach him, and he knew not what I knew but that I cared and really wanted to help him.

Today more than ever we have almost infinite options of what to learn and ways to learn, from various people and programmes. Not all of them know how to teach "pure" form, many have their own agendas, and at worst they are teaching incorrect and potentially destructive information.

Part of what this book is about and my goal for you is to have the Clarity to know what you want to learn and how you can learn and to see if you're actually making progress towards what really matters to you.

One final thought for now: "Don't confuse the teachings with the teacher." This idea has been attributed to spiritual teachers or philosophers over time, and for me today its exact origin is difficult to trace. It's a lesson I wish my younger self had learnt earlier as I lost too much time with charlatans who sold me on other people's ideas and were good at spinning tales. My younger self was impressed by their "stolen" wisdom as they made themselves the "guru". It's something that happens all the time today online with the latest young marketing "guru" selling the latest shiny tactic.

In fact, one of the challenges that held me back from writing this book and others over the decades is that I'd rather get on with helping people then spend time having to market myself and playing the game of trying to be impressive.

In the circles of the people that know, you'll find your character and legend will open the doors before you get there. Sadly, most people haven't really learnt to learn and take for granted what they read online or see on the TV or at an event.

So, keep asking yourself intelligent questions and commit to learning how you can learn optimally in ways that will serve you.

What I do believe is that your capacity to learn is far more than most people believe, and with new technologies arising you will most probably be able to learn more effectively and enjoyably than our ancestors ever dreamt. You'll also start to hear about "edutainment" more and more.

A final thought for now. Often, you're learning more than you realise and most often not just the subject you think you are learning. The best masters do this on purpose. I'm grateful for my experiences with them. Looking back, I have fond memories of those times. Chinese martial arts movies point at this more than most – Jackie Chan in the movie Drunken Master filmed in 1978 is a great example – also of the comedic nature at times of learning.

Whatever experiences you have – and you get to observe others having – and no matter what the learnings and planning beforehand, after the fact you get to do a review and enquire with hindsight, and in so doing learn lessons you couldn't have learnt ahead of time. If you can please avoid beating yourself up with hindsights as it really isn't useful or helpful or fair or kind. Regrets do weigh tonnes, as Jim Rohn said – it's more powerful to look at what valuable lessons you can get from the past to apply in the moment moving forward.

Nature is itself a great teacher – either by choice or necessity. Life is encouraged to learn to survive or perish and die. Nature can be brutal, but with numbers and chance there is always seemingly scope for growth and evolution. We'll explore the nature of nature in a later chapter. For now, it's worth pointing out that the lessons we learn and need to in the real physical world are often affected by the seasons and cycles of nature.

As an example, in the summer if we aren't aware that winter is coming, we may not realise the importance of saving for the hard times ahead. If we don't understand how seeds need to be planted in the spring if we want to harvest in the winter, we may find we're doing the right things but not producing the results because of timing and placement. The same constructions built on solid ground or sand will withstand the wind and rains and earthquakes very differently.

Nature has always been one of our ancestors' greatest teachers. Observations of the micro and macro can give us profound insights and approaches we can use in other realms of knowledge and application.

One of humanity's greatest polymaths was Leonardo da Vinci, and his approach to learning from nature was characterised by keen observation, scientific inquiry, biomimicry, and an interdisciplinary mindset. He would spend hours examining plants, animals, and natural landscapes, meticulously documenting his observations and conjectures in his sketchbooks.

These detailed drawings of human anatomy, animal locomotion, and plant structures are a testament to his dedication to understanding the natural world. In turn these learnings from nature not only enriched his understanding of the world but also influenced his artistic and scientific works. I glimpsed his focus and genius when I got to see his original sketches at an exhibition in London.

Today how few of us really journal and document our observations, let alone share our "scribblings"? If you're curious how to start doing this more, check out the Pause Stop Reset Yearbook

– which you can find at www.PauseStopReset.com/yearbook – which I designed exactly for this purpose.

How few of our children today put down the electronic screens to observe and sketch in this way?

I know I've learnt and grown and got real wisdom from often challenging (and even devastating) experiences. My Dad once said, "It's often the most expensive lessons in life that are the good ones." You can learn from others as well if you choose to take on a beginner's mind and really listen, but all too often it seems that we as humans are destined to have to learn the hard way.

Sometimes also it's only with time that we get to separate what happens from what we make it mean, and with the gift of perspective offered by time and space see things from a different angle.

As we watch young children having a tantrum, we get to imagine how it was for our own parents when we had ours.

When we start to teach others and share what we've learnt, we discover what we really know and what we "glossed over". When we start to teach other teachers – which may not happen for decades, if ever – then and only then we may discover other distinctions we never saw before. As someone who has been a committed student of multiple disciplines and a teacher for multiple decades too, it's only now at forty-five (both old and young) that I start to see and understand things I didn't even know were on the core curriculum.

Much of what can, and I would suggest must, be learnt if you truly want to move from Chaos to Clarity (and in many other areas worth exploring in life and business), does not live purely in the form of things which can be read in a book, packaged, and bottled. They have qualities – metaphysical – which are profound, and not just in the physical tangible sense. Simple examples are someone's commitment level and personal "why?". These things can't be bottled or put on a shelf wrapped up in a box with a neat little bow, but I have found that often they do make all the difference.

So now is a good time to take a little pause on this subject of learning to learn, and I'm genuinely curious what seeds are starting to sprout, what new insights and ideas. I also know we've planted some that will bear fruit as you read on and continue out in the world.

Thought Experiment:

If you were given a new game without any instructions – how would you approach it? How would you feel about the opportunity?

If you'd like to take this thought experiment and make it practical, I'd challenge you to play and complete "**Journey**", which is a computer game developed by Thatgamecompany. If you want even more "bonus" points, some extras are playing and completing it – without spending any money or looking up information about it – within seven days. This is something I recommended for many of my mentees and clients, and it's been quite profound the deep insights and learnings this thought experiment made real can open up.

The Key Questions:

As you move forward in life, I'd like you to come up with your key questions that you find add value to you and help you navigate from Chaos to Clarity.

These are some of the most powerful questions I think can unlock value for you in the area of learning:

1. What do I need to learn now?
2. What are the best questions I could focus on?
3. What have I just learned?

4. How can I apply this now?
5. How could I apply this in the future?

Summary:

We've covered this subject of learning and started to point to how we need to explore different ways of learning, choosing what to learn and even the success measures we bring to our learning investments.

So much of the world never considers this, and in the world we're in now and I predict will come to be in the next few years and beyond, we'll have more and more need to learn with a beginner's mind how we learn and what to learn.

Chapter 4

Assumptions and Expectations

> "The problem with making assumptions is that we believe they are the truth."
>
> — Don Miguel Ruiz

It's not what you know with certainty that will most trip you up in life, but what you know with certainty that isn't so.

So many areas of life ask us to keep being clear about the assumptions we make and not to make them. Especially in mathematics and science. Yet most people most of the time live inside a web of assumptions so complex that they would swear there are no assumptions.

Our distant ancestors had to navigate a chaotic and almost certainly a dangerous world. Imagine as they went into a new area of land, wondering what to eat. Would that mushroom nourish them or deplete them, or even kill them off? What about that water supply? Over time our ancestors would learn the rules of the game of the world they found themselves in and they made up rules to shortcut survival. They might see the consequences faced by members of their tribe when they eat red berries or red mushrooms, and based on their "negative" reactions assume that all red things would be dangerous and toxic.

You can fill in the rest here, I'm sure.

In our own lives we make up rules about what being a good friend is or how we should be in business and life in order to get by.

It's similar with expectations: our minds build on assumptions to fight the Chaos of our worlds and make "models" so that we can operate. We learn to expect things of ourselves and for things to happen, and when they do not, we get frustrated or worse. Many modalities including science ask us to not set expectations and to be in the moment. Yet like assumptions, it's almost impossible it seems.

What happens when you flick the light switch or press the power button on a computer?

Generally, we'd assume it works like others and the light would turn on or a computer would spring to life. We expect these basic mechanics of our world to keep operating the way they always do. Until they don't. The first time a lightbulb doesn't come on, we have to learn about changing a lightbulb. When the computer first doesn't turn on, we have to learn what to do and what to check that may have gone wrong. Hopefully we don't learn that we were assumed to have backed up our data properly by someone else, or that the backup we expected to work in the cloud actually didn't.

Sadly I've had those moments more than once in my professional career, and even when we had planned for disasters, the disaster recovery processes didn't always work. What about insurance, you say… well that's well and good when it does choose to pay – just not always as much as you expected. I promise you that the "no problem" claims process is rarely as smooth as it's sold to us. Really challenging is when you realise that even with all the money in the world, you can't recreate something you lost.

Most people haven't learnt mathematics rigorously and have misunderstood the nature of possibilities, probabilities, expectations, and experiences. Yet seemingly the world works, and many people live amazing lives.

How can we navigate life if we don't make assumptions or set expectations? Where do we have blind spots and limitations without even realising it?

Try on this idea as you read through this chapter: *"At best your information is incomplete and at worst inaccurate."*

Story:

Once upon a time in a far-off land a long time ago there were four blind sages. These sages were renowned as some of the smartest in all the world. People came from all over the world to meet them, ask them questions, and learn from their wisdom.

One day a traveller from a distant land arrived after an incredibly long journey and asked them what they thought of elephants. The sages were honest and admitted that none of them had ever seen an elephant, nor smelt them or touched them. They said that they could make stuff up based on the name, but in truth they didn't know at all, and they only liked to speak truth.

The traveller smiled at this and admitted that his own teachers had hoped that they would indeed admit what they did not know and in so doing reveal their true wisdom. He gave them great priceless presents, and as they thanked him, he told them that if they wanted, he could arrange for an elephant to be brought to them tomorrow.

As you can imagine, the sages were super excited and graciously accepted this kind offer, keen to increase their knowledge of the world. They also said they had very busy schedules, and only had a short window because of how many people were lining up to learn from them.

The sun was shining as the new day came around, and at the allotted time, the traveller arrived with the promised elephant. The sages were all invited to come forward to experience the elephant.

They heard its incredible noises and strong breathing. They all agreed it had a most unique smell.

Then they were invited to take a step forward and touch the elephant. Due to its size and its wild nature, the sages agreed that given their skills it would be best to be brief with their touch. Then the sages agreed to line up and do this together.

"As you wish", said the traveller.

As they stepped forward with their arms outstretched, the sages let out a gasp and a collective "aha" as their hands touched the elephant.

They stayed there for a minute feeling the elephant, and one by one their expressions of curiosity returned to their usual displays of confidence and serenity.

After a few minutes more the traveller asked, "Have you finished?", and the sages all smiled and agreed that they were. "Really, are you sure?", and again they confirmed that they were, so with that the traveller wished them well and promised to go and tell his teacher what had happened and to pass on their thanks.

Now the traveller was being polite; after all he wasn't a high-born noble, and it wasn't done to argue with the sages, so with a sigh he walked off on this long journey home.

You see, what had happened is that each sage had indeed touched the elephant. However, each had touched only one part of the elephant – the trunk, the flank, the leg, and the tail.

The sages, who knew they were smart and wise because they had been told so by everyone for so many years, all congratulated each other on what a wonderful few days and experience it had been, and they returned to their seats to await the next guest and answer their questions.

As you can imagine, all those in the area had heard the gossip and rumours of a new exotic animal – this elephant – visiting the sages.

At some point in the next few days, one of those queuing to meet the sages who hadn't managed to see it for himself, gave in to his curiosity and asked, "Please great sages, what was the elephant like?"

The sages smiled happy for the chance to share their newly gained wisdom, and spoke in turn but almost simultaneously:

- It's just like a snake – said the sage who touched the trunk.
- It's just like a wall – said the sage who touched the flank.
- It's just like a tree trunk – said the sage who touched the leg.
- It's just like a rope – said the sage who touched the tail.

Then this divine meeting with the sages started to turn into a chaotic hell – each laughing at the others for how foolish and wrong they were. This wasn't a small argument; after all, the sages knew from their own experience. They were adamant that they were right and the others were wrong.

In the crowd were some who had witnessed the elephant's visit, and they tried to help, saying "beloved sages, please don't argue; none of you is right: the elephant isn't really like any of those things. It's an amazing animal …"

However, that was as far as they could get before the sages all agreed that only those who had touched the elephant could possibly know what it was really like.

Eventually the crowds got tired of this farce and drifted off; the sages meanwhile never found a way to admit they were wrong, and they say that to this day, they continue to go around arguing with whoever will listen to them.

Meanwhile, the traveller eventually returned home to his teacher, and when the teacher asked him what he'd learnt, he said simply, "***We have a lot to learn, don't we?***".

Insights / Distinctions:

Let's start with some definitions from a mathematical context:

- **Possibilities**: These are the various potential outcomes or choices that may happen in the future.
- **Probabilities**: The likelihood or chance that a particular outcome will occur, often expressed as a percentage or decimal. A probability of zero means there is no chance that something can occur. A probability of one means there is absolute certainty something will occur (no chance that it won't occur).
- **Expectations**: The assumptions or beliefs that one has about what will happen in the future or how someone or something will behave. Mathematically this is a function of the possible outcomes and the probabilities that they occur.
- **Experiences**: The collection of experienced – i.e. they have happened – events, feelings, and perceptions that a person has lived through, often shaping their understanding of themselves and the world around them.

Assumptions must be useful or valuable, otherwise why would we have such a natural ability to make them?

Well let's not assume this to be true and try on what we call **Rule One – Assume Nothing and Confirm Everything.**

Assume nothing does not mean doubting everything, and learning how to be with and apply Rule One is an opportunity you can step into if you choose.

I come to my experience of it from my background as an auditor and in time an authenticator. Yet it remains one of the most powerful rules to live by if you want to have Clarity, and also one that I've found continually most challenging to operate by.

Personally, every time I've broken Rule One, the universe has taught me a lesson – often an expensive one.

Now that you know Rule One, you can try on if it's useful for you to use as a base foundation for your approaches moving forward.

Shall we get grounded in reality, inside this context of Rule One?

As you started to read the story at the start of this chapter about the four sages, did you start to assume you'd heard the story before? Did you find yourself going "that's not how it goes", or "that's not what I'd expected"?

(*P.S. as I re-read this section, I realise I'm assuming you actually read the story at the start of this chapter and didn't just skip to this bit. I'm also assuming you can read/listen, as otherwise you wouldn't be understanding what I'm communicating, and if you aren't then it doesn't really matter what I'm saying/sharing. If you haven't read it yet, pause and rewind and go back to the start of this chapter. What will you do now? It really can be exhausting trying to list out assumptions and handle them.*)

If you haven't heard it before, then you had the gift of beginner's mind. If you have and read it again, did you apply beginner's mind?

You see, this book is designed to produce a result for you, to give you an experiential learning to help you to really "***get out of your own way and remember what really matters to you***."

A couple of things in that statement I'd like to highlight: this is about you and for you and about who you are being and what you're doing now and into the future. You see, I can't possibly know all I'd need to about you as I write this book to perfectly diagnose and propose optimal ways for you to move forward. That would make me a psychic or an incredible statistician. However, as I shared in the Reality of Chaos chapter, I can't predict the weather, let alone your personal circumstance as you read this.

What I *can* do is provide information, insights, and enquiries which can help you understand the opportunity and the steps I've taken successfully with my clients and mentees and partners and friends, that may inspire your journey from Chaos to Clarity.

Have you ever found yourself thinking or saying, "I never thought I/you could do that", or "I never thought I/you would say that", or "No way, that's not possible."? That's a sign that assumptions and expectations of your inner/outer world had shown up as being off/incorrect/missing.

On the good days, these gaps/glitches allow for super positive powerful things to be experienced. On the bad/most challenging things happen which can be hurtful, damaging, and hard to navigate.

Despite all my experience, I've still tripped over assumptions and expectations more than I could have ever imagined I would.

At times I did my best to experiment and live with **Rule Two: Expect Nothing and Experience Everything**. As much as people operate with assumptions (and often false assumptions), they all the more operate with expectations (and especially false expectations).

It's quite fascinating when you realise how fragile the world is and how much of the Chaos we individually and collectively face and navigate is a function of the assumptions and expectations that without us realising limit our models of the world and our true understanding of what's possible.

So even if you manage to live by Rule One and Rule Two, considering more options is not necessarily a better approach. When we're building our ideas and predictions of what can happen based on false assumptions and expectations, then the more we consider what could happen, the more this can just lead us further down the garden path (as my grandmother would say). We can get stuck in paralysis by analysis – lost in our thoughts trying to plan and survive while days and years drift by.

This is a good point, I think, to take a moment to Pause Stop and Reset. New data and learning by its definition can be confusing as you start to let your powerful mind, heart, and spirit integrate it. This chapter has started to stretch a little our understanding of how we, others, and the world work.

Clearing a simple assumption or expectation that's been limiting you and your experience and results in the world can be truly profound. Be gentle with yourself and others as you start to do this, and give yourself and others time to integrate and optimise.

Thought Experiments:

The Countdown Experiment:

Get a timer – maybe on your smart phone – and set it for, say, 60 seconds. Then start the timer, close your eyes, and internally count down the time and guess when the timer is about to go off.

How do you think you'll feel about this experiment?
Do you think the time will pass quickly or slowly?
Do you assume this will be easy or hard?
Do you expect to guess early, late, or spot on?
What if you did this a few times; would your answers vary?
Whatever you notice or the result, are you able to not judge yourself good or bad?

You can repeat this with specific tasks, where rather than 60 seconds, you guess how long the task will take. This could be as simple as doing the dishes, or making your bed, or as complex as writing your next book.

Reflection Time:

Consider in your life when you yourself have realised that your assumptions about yourself, someone, or something weren't correct. On those occasions, how did you feel? Did you respond or react? Did you stay focussed optimally on what mattered to you in the moment?

Consider in your life when you had expectations about yourself, someone, or something that didn't get completed and exceeded. On those occasions, how did you feel? Did you respond or react? Did you stay focussed optimally on what mattered to you in the moment?

The Key Questions:

- What assumptions am I making?
- What am I certain of?
- How can I zero out my and other people's assumptions?
- What expectations do I have?
- What expectations do I have of myself?
- What expectations do I have of others?
- What expectations do I have of my equipment?

Summary:

In this chapter, we've started to explore with some Clarity the wonderful domain of assumptions and expectations, and the ramifications and real-world effect they can have.

Hopefully you've started to realise that most people are operating unaware of the assumptions and expectations that they live inside of, and so it's no surprise for you now to start to see how much they can impact your life and world and create almost infinite Chaos if you're not careful – even and especially when you don't want them to.

I know as I write this book that I risk being like one of the sages who touched the elephant, thinking I understand when in fact perhaps I've not even scratched the surface of what's possible.

As we wrap up this chapter, I'm reminded of, and I'd like you to try on, what it is said in summary that Socrates – one of the greatest ancient Greek philosophers – lived by as one of his core tenets – ***I know that I know nothing***.

Yet perhaps there are things you *do* know with as much certainty as you currently know is possible for you? Perhaps, "**Cogito, ergo sum**" – which translates from the Latin as "I think, therefore I am" – and was a dictum coined by the French mathematician and philosopher René Descartes.

In this apparent paradox is the opening to the possibilities of the world of Clarity.

I hope you can start to breathe and let go of some frustration and start to step into a space of fascination.

Life can be an incredible adventure, and in time we'll start to explore a possibility I like to call The World Quest™.

P.S.

Assumptions and Validation

People like people who validate them and their ideas, or at least pretend to.

This creates echo chambers, inside which people in Chaos can convince themselves that they are in Clarity.

People love to be in their comfort zones and to be in a state of certainty. Questioning assumptions and the status quo can often be uncomfortable and for many can feel "unbearably uncomfortable", so all too often people revert to their usual stance.

Chapter 5

Ontology

"You can never step into the same river twice."

— Heraclitus

Ontology is the art and science of being. It deals with the nature of being. One of the fascinating things about "Human Beings" is that it seems that most of our creativity has been harnessed externally into doing and having – not the being aspect.

It's said in the East that there are three mysteries: air to the birds, water to the fish, and being to the human.

This chapter on ontology will shine a light on this opportunity to step more into the possibility of Clarity and explore a space of enquiry and insight that can produce truly profound valuable results that impact being, doing, and having.

If you're familiar with ontology, then I hope this chapter will bring a warm smile, and if this is your first interaction with it, that it will inspire you as new worlds open up.

As you read on, remember what we've covered before, and consider how each distinction can apply here.

Story: The Three Stonemasons

Once upon a time there were three stonemasons working on a busy building site.

From the outside if you were observing and watching them, you would see them seemingly doing the same thing each day in the same way.

The stonemasons would each go and start with a large boulder and over days cut and shape it until it was just right. They would toil and sweat in the weather of the day – be it hot or cold, wind or rain. Only to repeat the process over and over again, day after day.

This is truly hard, detailed, and skilled work. The kind of work that takes a lifetime to master.

Yet in reality the stonemasons were quite different, and you would have thought in some ways that they were not doing the same thing at all, even though they were.

You see, one day a travelling dignitary came to inspect the work they were all doing on the large building site, which his employer had helped fund.

He was curious why the work reports were so different from day to day and from one worker to the next.

On the day of the inspection, it was scorching hot, with the sun beating down, and yet all three were hard at work.

He came to the first and asked him, "How are you getting on?"

The first stonemason growled and scowled back. Sweat coming off him, his face showed no pleasure as he grunted back, "How do you think I'm doing? I hate this, but what else could I be doing? It's crazy hot, and I'll be working flat out like this forever. My back is hurting, my hands hurt. Leave me alone, we weren't all born as lucky as some."

The dignitary was shocked, but rather than cause a fuss, he thanked the man, apologised, and walked on.

Coming on the second mason, he asked, "I hope you're not hating your job in this heat?"

The second stonemason put down his tools, turned, and smiled. "Why of course not. Yes it's hot, but it beats working in the rain and snow. My friends will meet me for a drink later and I can think of many other things I'd hate to be doing. I have a place to sleep tonight, have eaten well, and can pause for a moment to ease my thirst at the well. I can't complain."

With that he excused himself, went and got some water, and then got back to work.

The dignitary was relieved, and slightly surprised, as both masons had seemed to be similar and yet gave such difference responses.

So, as he came across the third stonemason, he half-heartedly bade good tidings to him and asked him how he was doing.

The third mason turned and shook his hand and smiled from ear to ear. "I'm so glad you're here and have come to see what we're doing. I am so thankful to be able to be here playing my part. What a glorious day we have as well."

The dignitary asked him how he was so upbeat and happy.

The third stonemason replied, "Why wouldn't I be? I know the work will take many years, perhaps it won't even be finished until long after I'm gone. However, I know I'm doing the work I can and playing my part in building a cathedral to celebrate God, and what better work could there be? Each day I have is a blessing, and even though it's not built yet, I can picture the children here a hundred years from now looking at these works in amazement, and that brings me joy."

Remember:

- It's not just what you do, but also your why.
- All the theory isn't worth an inch of experience.

- Experience over time can produce wisdom.
- Wisdom is far more precious and useful than knowledge.

Insights / Distinctions:

Two people can do something exactly the same externally, yet who they are being while they are doing it can be very different. They may produce similar results – or vastly different. What is certain is that their experience of what they were doing can be very different. That's a function of who they are being.

Let's use a simple example of doing the cleaning in a house and washing the dishes. One person can do it with a smile – happy to be helping create an amazing environment to be in that will nourish them. Another can do it with a grimace – angry, frustrated and more, wishing they didn't have to.

In the above example their being states – happy vs. angry – were visible on their faces. However, they needn't be. In fact, many people have become very good at keeping up a mask – so much so in fact they don't even know themselves.

We as humans in each moment can choose to be in response or reaction (or reflection). At work, when a colleague seems angry and says "not now", do you take it personally? Does it impact your mood? For many the answer is "yes". If you ask them why, they'd rattle off all their understandings about people and the way they are, and what that means. Yet the true impact is on them and their full self-expressions and freedom to be and create powerfully.

I won't mention their names, but several of my bosses in the banking space – while at PriceWaterhouseCoopers, Morgan Stanley, Royal Bank of Scotland, and ABN Amro – were really ineffective bullies. They, I'm sure, thought that they were doing the best they could to get the job done. Yet in truth they didn't inspire loyalty and respect, and most of us working for them did so from fear. They were happy – they got their bonuses. Was it really the best way to be?

I don't write this thinking I was and am always perfect in this area. Far from it, I'm human – yet I know this about myself, and I have made a commitment to myself and others to learn, grow, and be/do better.

I'm reminded of a saying I heard from a dear friend now no longer with us – the incredible Larry Mendez – who in my interactions with him had a brilliance in his eyes and ways of being that were quite extraordinary.

He shared with me that, "Human beings must be known to be loved. Divine beings must be loved to be known." A decade or so later, I realised and added, "And human beings forget that they are all divine."

I think we all want at our core to be our best. For me that's about being real, connected, collaborative, and creative. Yet we learn that we have to fight to survive. Some people learn that they can win by breaking agreements, circumventing, and being simply "unethical". The challenge I think is that not everyone has the same values, priorities, and beliefs about what's ok. I also from my upbringing and beliefs have some things that are definitely "bad" – lines that I wouldn't want anyone to cross.

For today let's keep the conversation light, though, as this is about you and your journey from Chaos to Clarity, and your opportunity to leverage ontology to help you with that.

Ontology is something that came naturally to me, and it also feels like an infinite kaleidoscope at times. When you realise that you have more choice than you thought, it can be super exhilarating. It can also feel like turning over pebbles at the beach, constantly looking for a new way to be to unlock something, get over a challenge, or create something more.

In time, what seems to come is the opportunity of the possibility of simply being – whether you call this presence, mastery, or some other term. Remember it's your journey and adventure. This is another tool in your toolbox on your journey from Chaos to Clarity. Also be gentle with others; most of the world as I write this has never even heard the word ontology, let alone had the luck to come across a pure-form expression of it.

Too much of the world today is full of people who care more about making a buck than making a difference. It's why I covered some of the things we did in prior chapters, and at this point I'd like to share one of my favourite quotes that hopefully points to why I and this book are different.

Consider the quote, "**Question anything anyone tells you, especially what I tell you.**" I've seen it attributed to Buddha and others, and it's one of those quotes that comes from the past, yet who actually sourced it I doubt I'll ever know with certainty.

You see, I want you to question, not go around saying, "Simon Says…" and being mini parroting robots. I want you to step into the lab of life and explore what's possible. Now you know you have the choice to, and that's the start.

One of the most fascinating aspects of our lives is that even in a still quiet room, we can be experiencing torments in the middle of our own minds, or be in any other state you can imagine and many you haven't yet.

Our experience of life is so profoundly distinct from just the "physical" elements. Whether this is all our dreaming delusions or reality beyond our ken is something philosophers and the greatest minds have explored for lifetimes.

Maui is always Maui. The island is the same, but your experience of the island is more a function of you, than her.

Personally, I choose to stand in the place of inquiry and exploration.

Thought Experiment:

You are super happy and excited and on the way to a party to celebrate you customised to your preferences.

As you head there you realise that:

1. You have a rip in your clothes, and they have got stains on them.
2. The route you were going to travel is blocked, and you can't get there.
3. There is no way you're going to make the party you've been looking forward to.
4. You have no mobile phone coverage so can't make any phone calls.
5. You have lost your keys and wallet.

Now even though this is just a thought experiment, did you start to react already?

If it did happen, how would you be being? What can you imagine you'd do?

However, if in that moment, you knew that everything was perfect and handled, how could you be?

Think about scenarios where you know you've overreacted – perhaps triggered from the past – and consider how you'd love to be in future situations knowing what you know now.

The Key Questions:

- How am I being now?
- How could I be right now?
- How do I want to be next?
- What can I be grateful for?

- What can I be excited and inspired about?
- How have I been being about the Chaos in my life?
- How have I been being about the Chaos in the world?
- How would I like to be about the reality of Chaos?
- How would I like to be about the possibility of Clarity?

Summary:

Ontology by its very nature is a subtle subject. It's an area of enquiry that can make all the difference. Who you're being and your view of your capacity to be responsible for your being is a treasure trove and, I believe, your birthright.

The distinction of Pause Stop Reset can be applied here, and often you'll be able to see where others are in reaction more easily than where you yourself are.

You'll see where their challenges at the "being" level are keeping them in Chaos – or even causing Chaos needlessly. This points to the beauty of having a great coach/mentor/teacher/buddy as they can help you see your blind spots (scotomas).

Each moment is an opportunity to be with the reality of Chaos and be with the possibility of Clarity in whole new ways. How you are impacts what you do – what you think, focus on, say, and do – and in turn in the results you produce and the experiences you have. These moments build step by step – almost certainly non-linearly – compounding over days and decades.

There is a lot of value and juice in your journey here, and I hope this chapter has whetted your appetite to explore, learn more, and apply.

DISCLAIMER & WARNING

When people start to become aware of new distinctions – especially ontology – often they fall into the trap of using them to "beat up" themselves/make themselves wrong – or worse, doing that to others. Be gentle and careful with your new insights and how/when you choose to leverage and share them if you do.

Remember – we never know what other people are going through. This doesn't mean we don't get to choose to shift and change. Others may not want, or be able to, or choose/decide to. That, some would say, is their right.

And the old schoolyard quote seems apt to bring up now:

"When you assume, you make an ass out of you and me."

Chapter 6

Priorities, Timing, & Schedules

"If you want to make good use of your time,
you've got to know what's most important and then
give it all you've got."

\- Lee Iacocca

I believe that gaining Clarity about your priorities and about what really matters should be one of your and our collective priorities. Prioritisation is a super valuable skill – yet few can explain how they really do it, let alone live optimally.

We live in a world that operates seemingly in the unique dimension of time. Being can shift in an instant. yet doing lives in time. Things take time.

How we think, and often are being, is a function not just of the circumstances we find ourselves in but also the time we think we have to accomplish all the tasks we believe need to be completed so that we can produce the results and have the outcomes and experiences we think we want.

That's a complex sentence and worth reviewing. It explains why often people act in ways that leaves us going, "people are weird".

In this chapter we're going to look at three distinct areas: priorities, timing, and schedules. They are so important, and yet after decades consulting to and with some of the most creative people, entrepreneurs, and businesses in the world, I'm clear most have no real idea about these things and what's possible when they're optimised. Equally the approaches used in the world often hide from and fight the reality of Chaos. The net result is a perception of Clarity that often descends into Chaos, with catastrophic effects.

I've also been lucky to spend time with incredible people who approach these subjects very differently to most and as a result create seemingly magical and extraordinary results.

Perhaps you will become or are already one of these. Either way this is the chapter where we'll explore how what matters to you gets to move from the world of possibility into the world of reality – and ideally with Clarity and certainty.

Story:

Your time starts now.

I'm sat in a cold-feeling room on an uncomfortable chair and at a creaking desk. A pile of lined paper sits on one side. A watch, a calculator, several black pens, a ruler, and a stapled question sheet complete the inventory.

Four hours lay ahead for this, one of the last of my professional accountancy exams.

When I finished university at Durham and put my pen down at the end of the last mathematics exams, I thought that would be the last time I had the experience of the "examination". Yet years later I was still facing the clock once again.

I had studied on top of the day job at PricewaterhouseCoopers, and rather than enjoying a warm summer in London with new colleagues and old friends, I was stuck inside poring over past papers and homework yet again.

The first time we had done a mock exam, all of us had run out of time, and basically failed. We hadn't learnt, the "professor" explained with a knowing smile, what it meant to be a professional and to prioritise and schedule that way.

What would you do with four hours and four questions. You have to answer all the questions to pass, so surely you just start with question one and get one with it?

Maybe you would read through and start with the hard question or the easy one first?

He smiled as he said that he would teach us to pass and that this is what we were to do: we were to take four separate pieces of paper, write our names and numbers on each, and clearly set out Question 1, Question 2, Question 3, and Question 4 on each in turn.

Then depending on what was being asked for – a report, a memo, a summary, a calculation, an opinion, we were to set out the templated framework headings for a generalised answer for each question in turn.

Then we had to be rigorous about answering each element of the frameworks so that none was completely blank.

The schedule and timing had to come first. The clock was king and judge and jury and executioner.

As a professional, the priority was being professional first and foremost. This meant you couldn't tell a client, "sorry we missed the deadline – we just ran out of time."

I may be explaining this shift badly, but over twenty years later it still surprises me how it altered my focus. This application of The Merlin Method has served me well.

Years later, I learnt to take the minutes and create action lists while in meetings and shortly afterwards. Why? Well if they weren't done there and then, they would never get created, and balls would be dropped.

Back in the exam room I kept looking at the clock, and the seemingly massive time of four hours, dripped away.

Yes, once the structure and schedule were in place, start with those things that were easy. Yet don't try and chop and change. Stay with the priority, one question at a time – blocking out worries about prior questions or what was to come.

All that mattered for those four hours was the exam and passing.

No thought of last weekend's television or future jobs, or anything.

Two hours in, and question 3 was begun.

One hour to go, and the last question started.

As the clock ticked down, I was finalising the last element of the last question.

As the invigilator boomed out, "pens down", I sat back in the chair and, like many in the room, took a deep breath.

Now all there was to do was wait for the results. They would be published in the newspaper in a few months' time. Fingers crossed.

For three years I had prioritised and scheduled my life around these examinations and becoming a qualified chartered accountant. As that examination finished there was nothing to do but celebrate with friends and be patient.

We had been trained by a professional training company who had helped hundreds of people qualify for decades. We had learnt to prioritise and schedule our work the way they said would work.

As I type this, I still remember the early morning arrivals at White Lion Street at Angel, the late nights, and the joy of hearing that myself and many of my work friends had passed.

Insights / Distinctions:

What are your priorities this very moment? Go on, think about it for a moment and think or say or write some of them out.

Now, whatever your mind came up with, did it include: breathing, engaging with this chapter, being where you were?

In each moment you can objectively know what you're prioritising as you're doing that (albeit possibly with other things in your head, splitting your focus).

This can be quite daunting when you realise that your current priorities don't match what you think they are.

Equally it's quite fascinating when you can be with the fact that so much of our world happens without our conscious control. Internally trillions of cells carry out their myriad of activities. Externally natural ecosystems eb and flow.

When we wake up in the morning, overnight billions of people have thought and done things we have no conscious awareness of. Millions of people may have died, and millions more may have been born. Yet we wake thinking the world is the same as when we went to bed.

We can create an environment – and in time behaviours – that cause us to focus on our priorities. Perhaps you already have some of that. Yet really this question of priorities is quite fascinating in that it's easy to make up priorities. However, to find those that stick and stay consistent over time seems impossible for many – especially in an attention-grabbing world that loves to throw shiny objects at us. Much of my life I've ended up doing things each day that I never imagined a decade earlier and often thinking I was "in charge" of myself. Does that resonate with you?

For this chapter I'm going to put aside mystical magical thinking and be mechanical and scientific. Can we agree that things happen in time – in periods of time, be they milliseconds or millennia? If something has no time to occur, then it can't occur. Things must be scheduled by us or by the chaotic universe if they are to occur.

Some people will talk about how things can manifest instantly – as if a single frame of a movie could change in front of you without any time changing. To observe this might take time. I'll leave you to be with that paradox. How can something shift in your observations if there is no time for it to shift? It would be like watching two movie scenes simultaneously. Fascinatingly these ideas are more and more explored and enjoyed by those exploring the idea of a holographic/quantum/vibratory field universe. But let's set aside these kinds of ideas, and ideas like circular time, for now for this chapter. Ok? Remember as we covered earlier, we're looking for distinctions and insights to be with the reality of Chaos and give us access to Clarity. I'm not asking you to believe anything I'm sharing as true, and in fact I'm specifically asking you to look at where you have assumptions and enquire for yourself.

So, if we want to be at cause in the matter of creating and experiencing those things that really matter, we have to schedule time for them to occur, and also for the things that have to be prioritised and accomplished in advance so that what really matters can become a probability and then a reality.

Let's take this book, Chaos To Clarity. I made it a priority to write a book and help people I know and hopefully many more I haven't met both now and into the future. The book was a priority and an idea for some time. It wasn't until I started to schedule the writing of the book, the editing, the review, the publishing, that it moved forward. You might be surprised at the timing and sequencing of the book writing and publishing process. For example, as I write this chapter, the front cover of the book has been designed, and we published blank books and built a website months ago. We got feedback on the cover and the design and the subtitle. My younger, less experienced self wouldn't have done that. It's also not necessarily the best order for everyone, but it seemed to work for me within the context of what mattered and matters to me now.

So much in life doesn't happen in the sequence and timing we expect. And if we remember the reality of Chaos, this shouldn't surprise you.

Yet if we really sit with that, it makes no sense to keep repeating the same processes expecting different results, yet almost all humans do this.

They are stuck in jobs and routines that don't produce the results they really want, and most people have things that matter for them that aren't complete.

For hundreds of years charities have wanted to make a difference. Yet the difference they want to make seems to never get completed – not once and for all.

For over twenty years, since I attended a workshop the weekend after September 11th in 2001 during which I realised something new was possible, I've been committed to "making the difference" such that no human has to suffer needlessly – without food, water, shelter or suffering from health challenges that can be solved. Yet I'm sad to say that globally the problems seem to be getting worse not better. Trillions of pounds of investment and billions of hours of human endeavour, and yet seemingly simple things are not yet complete.

My Clarity is that what matters to me doesn't yet matter to others in the same way.

My priorities aren't theirs.

I'm also clear that if I had taken different actions, I would potentially have been able to make more progress toward those goals.

Are you seeing how you can apply this?

Now let's bring these seemingly separate strands together powerfully. I'm going to summarise some of the work I did with incredible people who have worked in fields including space travel, the special forces, and global mega-scale events.

Let's use the example of Mission Control at NASA. For each mission, they know they have a clear priority for a mission to launch successfully, complete its objectives, and return safely home.

They have a plan and know the expected timing for each stage. They put in place buffers in case things take longer than planned.

They also think about all the things that could go wrong, and before they even launch, they do their best to think about how to navigate in these worst-case scenarios. Then they map out and document the timing and steps to follow. They have these back up plans ready to be scheduled via templates ready to go.

They do dress rehearsals and go over activities to bond as teams and get congruence and alignment on the priorities, timings, and schedules needed to achieve a successful project.

Now on the day of launch, do you think everyone is panicking all the time, running around like headless chickens? No, there is a space of calmness caused by all the work that's been done to create room for the possibility of Clarity.

Do the people running these Mission Control rooms go looking for distractions and try and multi-task? No, they turn off distractions and go into specific environments, doing their best to set themselves up for success.

They also put in place redundancies – ideally duplicated or triplicated systems. Backup generators. Printed out physical notes and workbooks not reliant on electronic systems.

Yet sadly even with all this, there is still danger and challenges. Things go wrong. New explorers step out of comfort zones, and no matter how much we plan, there are always going to be those things you could never have planned for.

The challenge I'll put to you is this: for those things that really matter to you today, how many of them have you invested the time doing strategic planning for? How many of them have documented priorities, schedules, and timings? Do they have backups and redundancies?

As I write this, I'm present to how despite working on this for over a decade, most of what matters to me still doesn't have the level of rigorous structures I'd love. Why? Partly because I've found it hard to find the people I can trust and train who have the ability to step into roles I would need them to.

Partly because as I keep moving forward, there are new conversations, opportunities, technologies, people, and projects emerging seemingly from nowhere.

However, I can also reflect that a lot more is in place than was there a decade ago.

It's also true that while writing this chapter was my priority and what I scheduled to do, I had an unexpected incoming call from one of my old VIP clients. She rang the bat phone and greeted me with a cheery hello. It was her first call to me in months, and years since she's called me on a Tuesday lunchtime, so I wasn't sure what the call was about. I prioritised her – people matter to me – and listened fully for a few minutes until I started to understand not just what she was saying, but why she was really calling. Now, thirty minutes later, I'm back to the writing. The schedule I set was flexible enough, and in some ways the call was perfect as an example of what happens that takes us off from just focussing on our priorities and completing our plans. Some would call it a distraction, others divine timing. For me it was a choice to take her call or not. Had today's writing been mission critical (and perhaps it was), then I know I could have turned off the phone and all notifications and gone into bat cave mode.

In life we'll rarely know what would have been more optimal priorities and schedules until we look back with hindsight. That hindsight is rarely perfect.

Now, why else do we struggle as humans to cause and create what really matters to us?

Here in England, we originally championed timing and a central clock time in order for trains to run on time, and people to have schedules to plan their days, lives, and business around. Yet anyone who's ever travelled on English trains knows that all too often the trains don't keep to their schedules. Trains break down, leaves on the line, train strikes, people not using the trains as intended… the list goes on. So if we can't manage that despite all our collective skills and focus, what hope is there, right? Well I'd suggest that it's simply that making sure there are always trains running on schedule isn't really the top priority – not for everyone.

There is no national dashboard and scoreboard of the outcomes and all the key metrics that would make it likely or not. There isn't the top and exclusive news of train delays and new research. Scientific research isn't only focussed on this one goal.

That would be silly, right?

Assuming we know what our priorities are, they can seem to conflict. Say, for example, that I would love to live in nature and teach tai chi every day. I can't live in China and learn to speak and write fluent Mandarin while also living here in the UK and being there day to day for my existing clients, or be travelling the world advising governments on global goals projects, or be working with female founders to help them build their wealth and reach.

So our ability to have multiple priorities – or inability to have a single priority and focus – is one of both our greatest gifts and our greatest challenges.

Even if you are able to come up with a single, clear grounded priority that is real and true for you, you may have no idea of what actually needs to be done, let alone scheduled, in order to make it a reality. Even if you do have a clear idea that is 100% accurate on what needs to be scheduled and the timing of those sequences, you may find you don't have the capital and resources to carry that out.

Capital and resources aren't just about money – though often people think the money is the constraint. It also includes raw materials, technologies, skills and capabilities, physical spaces, and most importantly other people and their health, energy, creativity, and commitment.

I'm sure you know someone who has struggled to accomplish a simple task. Worse, they've worked with someone who used up the time and resources available, but what was done wasn't just sub-optimal, it was worse than if nothing had been done at all.

These judgements about what is a good and bad use of resources in a world that is more and more distanced from direct physical survival are based on a snapshot of perceived assumptions and expectations. As we've already touched on, assumptions are rarely useful.

Imagine a parent or teacher responsible for a young child. They may think there are different priorities than the child, who may just want to eat sweets and play games. We'd probably all think the parent or teacher knows best. Yet even in that dynamic it's not always so cut and dried, is it? So what possibility is there for real Clarity around priorities in a world where we coexist, and ideally learn to collaborate with others, and where there are billions we don't consciously have a real relatedness with.

So many of the great successful endeavours of our human species we look back on and realise never really mattered. We wonder why people ever did things that way for so long. This is the joy of the technology revolutions.

Some of the largest companies are filing for bankruptcy, lives given over to chasing money and financial gain, only to result in global conflicts.

Focussing on you, what matters to you today may change over time. When you get the Clarity on what really matters, then you can choose to navigate the world. You can take responsibility for how you prioritise your time and resources. How you schedule things. And how good you get at knowing how long you will take to complete things and giving yourself and others buffers.

You'll also get better at seeing the potential consequences of saying "yes" and "no" to things. As you get clearer about what really matters to you, you may choose to say no to things you used to say yes to, and yes to things which you used to say no to. You may also find that as you make your choices, you know they aren't optimal, but you still decide them because of other situational contexts – e.g. "I don't really want to do that low-paying work today; that isn't my highest use of my time, but it will enable me to pay for an emergency repair I need and I may not have anything else readily available."

Your tolerance for being with the ontology of these choices and their consequences can be very profound. Having a "day job" as an employee in banking for a decade was very stressful a lot of the time, but it was nothing compared to the emotional roller-coaster of working for myself the following decade.

All you can do is this week, this day, this moment get present to your priorities, and using all your insights, tools, distinctions, and wisdom choose where you navigate to next. This may also include taking a pause and allowing yourself to be centred and grateful – to rest and recover until you have the Clarity on the next most likely step to take.

Then like a master samurai, when it's time to act, you act like lightning. You put your all into what you are doing and who you are being.

Windows of opportunity will arise and fall. Often out of nowhere, and often outside of your control.

You can be prepared and ready to act, and also discern if this is one you'll choose to jump through or not.

The fact that you have space to read and think about these things means that almost certainly you are not in hyper-crisis mode. If you know you need drinking water in the next 60 seconds or you'll die, then that has to be your highest priority, right? There are other requirements for survival – water, food, and shelter being some of the top three. There is a large percentage of the global population operating from crisis, hyper-crisis, or triage.

In those contexts, surely the ability to choose is affected? Being able to breathe and be safe can seem like such natural states. Yet in fact for many they really are not a given state at all. Don't take your current good fortune for granted, and being present to and grateful for the positive things in your favour is, I believe, essential if you want to really move from Chaos to Clarity. Your capacity to think and be creative is one of those.

Nil desperandum.

Let's continue…

I remember one of my dearest recent clients; she had a priority to speak in public so she could really make a positive global impact. However, she hadn't had much experience as a professional speaker and had no real track record of speaking at large 10,000+ people events. We'd thought through her subjects and how she might speak, and the ideal stages and events she'd love to speak at. Then one day as we were doing a session about this very subject, her phone rang, and it was an event organiser.

They seemed apologetic and then asked pleadingly if she could possibly speak as the major keynote as the original booked celebrity speaker had just bailed on them with no notice. This was a clear opportunity, and she said yes to them with a smile while containing her surprise and excitement. After she ended the call, she screamed with delight. She couldn't believe it, and yet like the mission control teams we'd planned for this moment and set up conditions to allow it to emerge and for her to take action towards her real goals.

Where in your life have you been blocking yourself from stepping into what matters? Where do you not have the space scheduled to work on what matters to you or for it to show up?

Sadly, some of the so-called influencers of the personal development and business world have great marketing and PR teams – hiding the real craziness of their internal and business worlds. They are often busy busy busy, and not leading lives you'd want to copy. I often realised this too late, having spent years getting to know them. A decade plus well invested?

I hope so, but at times I have big regrets, which I really don't wish on you. Finding yourself going "if only I'd done A rather than B" can be very difficult to process and live with. Yet it's the human condition.

So, think carefully who and why you choose to emulate around priorities, timing, and schedules.

You get to decide what matters to you – and to reassess it.

Once you have, make it a priority, and allow yourself and your life to be shaped by it.

Thought Experiments:

The Talent Contest

Imagine one of those televised talent shows, with the celebrity judges deciding good or bad.

The next candidate comes on stage, nervous and excited. They believe they are good. They had prioritised practising their talent for years. They had made a huge commitment to practise daily, for hours at a time. They got up early and stayed late working on their talent.

They didn't go on holidays or watch movies. They didn't make lots of friendships or have a great personal life. The skill they were developing had to come first. They had clear priorities and commitment to see it through. They worked hard to find the money to get equipment and training.

They start their act with a smile, and not even halfway through, a buzzer is pressed, and the judges all declare, "Stop… enough!".

Then they follow up with, "What are you doing? You're useless. That's the worst ever. This is never going to work out. Give up. Don't waste your time. Big No!".

How would that candidate feel?

Should they thank the judges for the honest feedback or storm off angry and disagreeing?

What would you do if you were that candidate?

Where the judges right? And if so, was their years of practice a waste of time?

Should the candidate give up their interest and practice?

This thought experiment up to now highlights a few things to consider:

- The paradox of the person's dedication to their skill not necessarily equating to success or recognition.
- The importance of honest feedback and assessment to improve and adjust priorities and schedules.
- The question of "Is it a danger or a requirement to have a singular focus on something for years?"
- The risk of putting all eggs in one basket, potentially sacrificing other important aspects of life.

Now then:
How would your thoughts alter if a few years after they got the judges' ruthless feedback:

a. They came back and were a big hit. Being told they were awful had spurred them on to prove the judges wrong.
b. They kept practising for the rest of their life and were never "any good". People kept laughing at them and thinking them crazy. (*Here consider, "Do you practise for others or yourself?"*)
c. They never practised again. They found a new passion for friends and a new calling which they poured their energy into and over time built a life others would judge as "successful".
d. They never practised again. They lost their spark for life and carried on a "normal", unremarkable life.

Hypotheticals

This is a simplified version of some of the questions I've asked my Strategic Alchemy clients over the years. The questions helped them get Clarity about their priorities and what could matter to them.

- Hypothetically, if you had only 24 hours left on planet Earth, how would you want to spend your time?
- Hypothetically, if you had £500 million pounds in your bank account tomorrow morning, what would you do with it?

A Penny Walk

Next time you have time for a walk or journey, and you can do it safely, then consider doing a penny walk. This is where when you get to a junction in your route, you decide whether to go left or right based on the toss of a coin.

Normally when you walk, how do you prioritise going left or right? How much can that affect your experience? The other day I turned left on a penny walk and I met an old friend I hadn't seen in nearly twenty years – they just happened to be visiting the town where I'm living and had no idea I was there, and vice versa. If I had turned right, I might never have seen them. I find the real treasure in life is made up of these "you couldn't make it up" moments.

The Key Questions:

- What are your priorities?
- What were your priorities a decade ago?
- What would you love your priorities to be a decade from now?
- What do you have scheduled today?

- What do you have scheduled a decade from today?
- Do you set the timing for your life or does someone/something else?

Summary:

As we wrap up this chapter, I'd like to leave you with some simple ideas and insights:

- If you don't prioritise what matters and you don't schedule what matters, don't be surprised if you don't get to produce and experience what matters to you.
- Just because you do prioritise what matters and schedule what matters… this doesn't mean you'll get to produce and experience what matters to you.

What I hope you'll start to be excited about is that as you get greater and greater Clarity about what really matters to you now and into the future, your ability to be clear about what your priorities are and how you prioritise in each moment can increase. Without clear context and outcomes, there can be no clear priorities.

Clear priorities allow you to get clearer about what needs to be scheduled, and what is and isn't yet scheduled.

This in turn will help you get greater Clarity on the importance and your capacity to Pause Stop Reset your and others' schedules. In time you can become a master of timing – that can seem almost magical.

This is when what I call Strategic Alchemy starts to open up. Those moments when you're in such flow, with such synchronicity that it truly can feel like the world is working with you, not against you.

Some of the most successful people I know of – in terms of results production and also their expressions and quality of life – have a mastery of these aspects that others don't think is even possible.

So, will you choose to prioritise this now? Will you schedule time now to reflect?

Will you schedule some time this week, and every month moving forward?

What if you did?

Bonus Opportunity:

One of the tools I built for myself and my clients is an app available for the iPhone or iPad called iPrioritize. You can learn more about it at www.i-Prioritize.com . The app helps you take your goals and prioritise the steps you come up with to achieve them.

It's made a huge difference to lots of people and while super simple in concept, it can save a lot of time and help you build momentum. It also gives you a place to start when you're not sure, and an example of how you can move from Chaos to possible Clarity around these subjects very quickly when you choose to.

Bonus Story

A great chef had been training his apprentices for many years. It was finally time for the chef to retire, and to celebrate, all the great and the good were going to come for a wonderful feast.

The apprentices were excited, especially as the chef announced that at the feast would be a contest, and the winner would inherit his restaurant and be the new "boss".

On the day of the feast, everyone was amazed.

There were the most sumptuous of dishes, and such variety that everyone could find something to their liking. The chef cared about people, not just accolades, so he made sure food was given to everyone that asked and even to those who hadn't dared come into the feast, thinking they weren't good enough. In fact, by the end of the feast there was nothing at all left in the larder.

It was truly a magnificent and masterly display.

Eventually as the last of the guests departed full and with their "doggy bags" overflowing, the apprentices murmured then finally nudged one of juniors to ask the chef, "What about the contest?"

He smiled. "You thought I had forgotten? Of course not, but as a chef you must take care first to feed your guests and make sure they leave happy. Now the last has gone home we can take care of business. First, let's get the room tidied and the kitchen squared away. I'll be watching, and yes the contest has begun."

The apprentices groaned – they had been preparing food and practising for months for this amazing feast. However, chef was chef, and they didn't want to lose out, so they got to tidying and cleaning like their lives depended on it.

It was nearly sunrise when the chef finally smiled and said, "ok that's enough; so who knows the secret to cooking a perfect roast chicken for today's lunch?"

One cocky apprentice spoke up. "Chef, I know, I know… let me go first. I have watched you for years, and how I would cook it is…" He continued to share his ideas full of spices and flavourings and more.

Another took out his notes and very scientifically talked about how he'd brine a chicken for 12 hours, then roast it for 3 hours turning and basting it then let it rest.

Another talked about using a special rotisserie machine.

Each in turn shared their recipes, some turning to their notes and others making up ideas on the spot. Each trying to shine.

Finally, the quietest apprentice – in fact the dogsbody, as the others thought of him – was asked by the chef what he thought, and he said, "Well those all sound amazing chef, I'm sure they could make a wonderful meal fit for a king."

The chef pushed him. “What about you; how would you go about cooking me the perfect roast chicken for today’s lunch?”

The dogsbody paused and double-checked, “for today’s lunch?” The chef nodded.

“Well, the first thing is, I’d have to go catch a chicken…”

The chef smiled and stopped him there. “Congratulations. I’ve found my successor. I’m glad one of you was paying attention.”

To this very day, in this award-winning restaurant, the first step in their secret recipe to cook the perfect roast chicken says:

“STEP ONE – FIRST CATCH YOUR CHICKEN”

Chapter 7

Nature of Nature

"Nature does not hurry, yet everything is accomplished."

— Lao Tzu

So much of the modern world and our human lives is abstracted from the very fabric of the world and universe we find ourselves born into. We are part of nature, yet seemingly we do our best to forget this or are encouraged to.

Ancestrally we all had to source water, find shelter, and navigate the challenges of the wild while making it a priority to hunt and gather our food. This was a daily activity that only civilisation in its various forms started to shift.

I know I have happy memories of picking fruit – strawberries, ripening plums, and wild blackberries on the hedgerows; the shocking sight of caterpillars munching away on the cabbages and pulling up potatoes, shaking off the soil, in my small kitchen garden; being present to the seasons and the needs of those seasons to work with them. Nature was in charge.

Yet, those days are decades ago for me.

What about for you?

How many of us have always grown all our own food, let alone recently?

In this chapter we'll look at the nature of nature, and how this paradox of being part of nature and yet forgetting it may be more important today and in the years to come, especially as you focus on remembering what really matters.

Story: Snow

12th December 2022 - Yesterday the snow fell.

I've seen snow before, and it is December and I'm in England, so this isn't not normal.

Yet the country seems shocked. Airports and roads closed. Schools closed.

As my brother was driving home less than a few miles from his destination, he chose to pull in, and was grateful he did as ahead of him at least five cars collided with each other while trying to navigate a normal road in un-normal conditions.

This isn't the first time we've experienced snow as a country, and yet it seems to have caught people unaware.

For some it's their first experience of snow.

For others it's their first time in their current roles in their current organisations when people are dealing with a reality that is not a scenario mapped out in an operations manual.

While the usual seasons of spring, summer, autumn, winter seem to be continuing and Christmas is just a few weeks away, somehow the minus-five-degree weather and the sudden snowfalls have caught us unawares.

This despite all the time and money invested into weather forecasting systems and smart AI technologies designed to make things better, and more predictable.

How can this be the case?

Elsewhere in the world, this would be a business-as-usual day, but here it really isn't.

Equally we're now expecting more strikes from train staff and other unions – including the NHS – as people try and get a better deal to handle the fact that the economy is spiking into inflation and also a recession yet again.

Events planned a week, a month, a year, and even a decade ago now seem so disrupted they would need to be cancelled, if that was even possible.

Yet today I'm able to sit and write this and think about you reading these words and engaging with this book and feel somewhat content.

I'm grateful for the warm blankets on the bed, and the laptop that's working that is enabling me to write.

Yet if you'd asked me even a few hours ago, I would not have expected to be writing these words today.

I'm also processing some things that have happened in the last few weeks that I won't share the details of – to honour the privacy and grief of the people involved.

I'm reminded of the fragility of life, and the importance of what matters to me now is different than it was even a few months ago.

Sometimes I've felt like I have the answers, and then at others I am present to the awe-inspiring nature of reality and do my best to breathe and be present in it.

In this book, Chaos To Clarity, I'll explore more with you with a singular focus – to provide a space and bridge for you that can make a difference for you.

Earlier tonight I was talking to one of the people I've most invested time and energy with over the last few years, and we talked about the question of what's **really** valuable and useful.

In recent weeks and years, multiple "flagship" success story multi-billion-dollar businesses and entrepreneurs have been proven to be frauds and criminals. With my background as an auditor, I understand all too easily how this can happen and am shocked that in today's technological age it has still been allowed to go on.

There are clearly aspects of human behaviour both at a macro level and a personal level where we can see patterns (at times).

Yet sometimes, like the tracks in the snow, even when we see the tracks we see, it's hard if not impossible to imagine, let alone be certain, what's caused them. Unless it's ourselves. I'm thinking about the serpentine tracks in the snow in my back garden that had my mind wondering what kind of snake could have made them, or perhaps something else like a vole.

In truth with those specific tracks I'll never know, and that's ok.

However, for the wider aspects of what I'd urge you to notice, there are more and more signs of Chaos showing up in the world and in people's everyday experience of what it means to be alive.

We may not notice the first snowflake, but after a night of heavy snowfall when the weather is cold enough, it's hard not to notice the crisp white snow as you step outside into the real world.

That millions of people literally woke up saying, "Oh wow, it snowed. When did that happen?" is an interesting thought.

So, where to now?

That is a good question, and for me it's time to pause and wrap up this story and leave you with this… The truth is, it doesn't much matter where you're going unless you have some preferences and priorities, and an awareness of your current capabilities and resources.

Soon it will be a new day and the journey begins again.

24 hours.

86,400 seconds.

Will the snow be there when I wake up? We'll see.

Insights / Distinctions:

As I stated at the beginning of this chapter, the importance of being present to the nature of nature and its qualities may be more important today and in the years to come.

As our world becomes hyper-connected, and we seem to lose our understanding of the old ways, we become reliant on other people and services more and more. We are seeing more and more centralisation and "optimisations" as larger groups come together. Yet this means that knowledge, resources, and the key ingredients for natural success become strained.

Here in the UK and in many other places, the cost of land has rocketed, meaning that even with millions of pounds you couldn't acquire the space you'd really need and might want to build a self-sustaining life.

We see agriculture requiring huge amounts of machinery and specialised fertiliser and being more at risk from pests and outside dangers. Blights and worse requiring whole farms to be wiped out – for the greater good – are a common occurrence.

Certain strains and species have been wiped out altogether, and this is likely to continue occurring.

During the last few years, we have seen supply chains crippled seemingly unexpectedly and the cost of food and basic essentials skyrocket.

Here as I write this, we are expecting the summer to be hotter than ever, and no matter what your thoughts on the great climate challenge, it cannot be said that weather is moderate everywhere.

Floods and famines have been all too present in my lifetime, and they are likely to continue. Yet most of the world isn't truly prepared for this.

It's like we as a collective species choose to live in denial to the reality of nature.

Recent news here in the UK has been highlighting villages and towns being affected by coastal erosion. Photos from sometimes less than a decade ago show hundreds of metres of land lost to the sea. This isn't new. The land and sea have been dancing together for millennia, shaping our world. Yet we rarely consider this when we build. We like the view and the benefits.

Someone else's problem perhaps, or simply naïve buyers and unscrupulous builders.

Elsewhere properties regularly have had to deal with earthquakes, mudslides, and more – often destroying not just millions in property but real human lives that can't be insured or replaced.

Does this feel like bad news? I hope not, and I'm also doing my best to give a wakeup call.

When I worked in the City, I would often arrive in the office at Canary Wharf before sunrise and leave after sunset. The climate was controlled inside. Air conditioning and electronic lighting. The occasional potted plant to remind us of the real world. Food eaten in the canteen. Many days not seeing the sun at all. Why choose to work this way? There are many humans globally working in far worse conditions. Generally, to earn money so that they can survive. Perhaps so "we can". More likely because it serves some.

I'm reminded of the works of Buckminster Fuller, and his Clarity and that of others over a hundred years ago that we could all – yes every one of us – live on spaceship Earth with the quality of life of billionaires, and with no one left out and without damaging the environment. A beautiful vision for the world that he inspired many, including me, to work towards. What has to happen for his vision to become a reality? He would say "integrity" – individual and collective – and also, I believe we have to learn to really collaborate and get real about things that up to know we've chosen not to.

Nature really doesn't care about most of the works of humankind.

I'm shocked as I get older how the building we live in and the way the "human" world has been built is seemingly at war with Nature and definitely not working with it.

The signs of this are so clear that it's hard to miss them, yet we seem to keep repeating the same things expecting different results – insanity. A simple example can be seen on the road surfaces here in Kent, which after freezing winters and hot days are so full of gaping potholes that what should be a simple journey becomes an advanced driving test, and countless vehicles have suffered massive damage.

Even more widely seen is the way in which properties left unlived in are reclaimed in months and years, not decades. Even lived in, people are fighting off mould and movement. Cracks appear that need constant touching up. Are we naïve to imagine that our constructions would work for life?

Our ancestors somehow built differently – at least in places. You can come across ancient caves where the rocks still display the marks of ancient fires and the whispers around them. Pathways through forests and across the moors and hills that snake from vale to vale.

Are you starting to realise how much of modern life ignores nature?

Some may say it doesn't really matter. Perhaps it doesn't matter where the food and water come from, just that we have it. What about the way our technology and energy use the minerals found deep inside the Earth?

All too often it's not until it's too late that we realise the impact we have on nature and the way it's not a bi-directional choice for us.

The amount of waste – in all its forms: conventional, toxic, nuclear, and beyond – will ripple through our interconnected ecosystem for generations. Much of it hidden and lied about. Stories you can look into or may know well, such as the "Flint Michigan" water disaster or "Dark Waters", I predict are just scratching the surface.

Does ignorance help? Not really. Too many people have eaten food and drunk water they thought safe only to realise the consequences years later.

So, what do we do about this?

I believe we can choose to apply the distinctions we've explored earlier when we start to consider nature. We can start to choose to focus on what's important and really matters to us in these areas, and from that perspective increase our enlightened self-interest.

I don't have all the answers, but I do know that nature has surprised me more than I ever imagined, and if you want to really move from Chaos To Clarity™, you need to get present to the nature of nature.

Thought Experiments:

The Weather

Imagine an event you are looking forward to.

Does the weather outside have any impact on the ability of the event to happen, or your enjoyment/experience of it?

Are there workarounds or backup plans that could make the event the same no matter what the weather?

Where have you been surprised by this in the past?

Where has this "chaotic" aspect of nature impacted your plans?

Emergency Lockdown

Imagine the power went out and you had no running water or electricity for the next seven days; could you survive without leaving the space you are in now? What about 30 days?

What would you really need to survive? What would be nice to have? What would enable you to thrive? Does money play any part in your thinking? What if you had a very tight budget? What if you had a limitless budget?

I'm curious – did you include other people in your thinking or wish list?

What if this continued for six months or more?

Survival Mode

Imagine you find yourself out in nature – you can imagine the scenario. Somewhere near where you are now.

Could you survive? What would you need to focus on and in what order?

What could you make do without? What would no longer matter?

Do you know where to find fresh, safe drinking water?

What real dangers – not imagined – would you have to navigate each day?

How would this change in different seasons of the year?

The Key Questions:

- Are you living in synchronicity with nature or oblivious to it?
- Is the world and life you and others are building more or less likely to be affected by nature now and in the future?
- What would happen if nature's cycles, seasons, and patterns change? How ready are you for that?

Summary:

Some of this reminder about the nature of nature should come as no surprise. After all, you've grown up as part of nature and witnessing it go through many changes and cycles.

We could invest years exploring this subject, and as you continue reading on and considering what really matters, consider nature and if it could become an ally rather than an enemy.

Chapter 8

Intentions and Outcomes

"Align your intentions with the flow of the Tao,
and the outcomes will effortlessly fall into place."

— LSH, Shibumi Master

At some point, whether in Chaos or Clarity, you will see something you want to change, make a difference with, or transform. You can then muster your will and increase your focus and intention towards these new possibilities and realities.

Intentions can be defined as the conscious and deliberate mental states or attitudes that guide one's thoughts, actions, and decisions. They represent the purpose, aim, or desired outcome behind one's thoughts or actions, reflecting their underlying motivations and desires.

Intentions often play a significant role in shaping behaviour and influence the direction and focus of our efforts and lives. They can provide a sense of direction, Clarity, and meaning to our actions and can impact the way individuals interact with others and the world around them.

Intentions live in the inner world. They are metaphysical. They're not easily – and perhaps not at all – able to be measured objectively with 100% accuracy by others, and potentially not even by ourselves.

Much of our life and the actions of humans is driven by these "whys".

We do X intending Y, and we experience Z.

Outcomes can be defined as the consequences, or end results, that occur as a result of a particular action, event, or process. For some people outcomes are only the observable or measurable effects or achievements that result from a specific action, endeavour, or set of circumstances. For this chapter, however, consider all possible outcomes – those that are observable and those that are not (or at least not yet) observable. Outcomes can be positive or negative, intended or unintended.

Often we measure success and what's good based on a temporary snapshot of the sliver of outcomes we perceive.

Intentions and outcomes are very distinct and rarely as correlated as we'd like, and we'll look in this chapter at why and how this can be. We'll also explore some of the aspects of intentions that may not be obvious and yet may make all the difference, especially in the adventure from Chaos to Clarity.

Story:

It was a key day that I'd been working towards for years. Meetings I'd scheduled months in advance at the flagship Apple Store in Covent Garden in the business briefing room, for some of my top VIP clients, and more events scheduled later that day at The Shard at London Bridge, starting with a breakfast briefing and running through till midnight.

I intended for it to be a breakthrough day and a day that changed everything for the better, with new joint ventures being formed that had been years in the planning.

I intended to arrive early – after all, on time is late in those worlds. I had run the routes many times and dress-rehearsed the events countless times.

The day before, I got asked to come to a final check-up meeting out of town and agreed. I was told that there was essential strictly confidential information that I had to know about, and which could only be told in person. So off I went, arriving at 7pm for what I expected would be a few hours of briefings. "Trust me," they said, "you'll definitely be there on time, I promise you."

Fast forward and it was now 2 a.m. and I was getting conscious of the time. It was too late to return to my base in Central London, so the suggestion of kipping down for a few hours on the floor with the promise of a warm blanket, while not ideal, seemed like a workable solution. My gut was saying it would be ok – not ideal, but workable.

The next morning at 5am, I had a shower and waited for the taxi to take us back to London. I had prebooked it the night before just in case. It arrived on time and off we went; we'd be there by 7am; 8am at the latest – all in time for the intended events and carefully curated itinerary.

Thirty minutes later, the motorway was bumper to bumper, and the rain was coming down in sheets. An unexpected flash storm. "Don't worry," says the driver, "I know a short cut." Plenty of time still; after all, we had a buffer and others on the ground who could manage things.

Suddenly the driver is heading down strange country lanes that kept twisting and turning and shrinking to single lanes. I'm holding onto the handle for balance. Thrilling it seemed, until turning back onto the only route we could take, we're back in bumper-to-bumper traffic and signs saying, "Road ahead flooded and closed."

At this point, it was clear we wouldn't make the early breakfast meeting, so I went to call my team on the ground. No signal. Strange – we were in a prime coverage area. I checked my other phones and the same thing. I had with me three of the latest iPhones at that time with multiple battery packs because of the importance of being able to stay in communication with all that was happening.

The signal would come back in a few minutes, right? So I waited. Yet every time I checked, the phones had no signal. No matter what I tried, my phones had no coverage. I turned them off and on again – no difference.

I asked the driver if I could borrow his phone, and *he* had no signal. The others in the taxi, same thing.

So now I'm stuck in traffic with no clear end in sight or way to turn off or get to a train station and, despite multiple phones and multiple networks, no way to make any calls.

I finally got to The Shard at 3pm, and I'd love to say I was fascinated by the experience. Worse, some of the people who we had scheduled to meet where only in London for the morning; they had already gone on their travels. Not every outcome can be recreated.

It turned out that the phone networks – including O2 – had had a major breakdown, and the network had been down for millions of people.

Had it just been the phone issue, we could have communicated by email or landline. However, with the meeting I just had to attend (a three-line whip meeting, as they say) and the unexpected traffic and weather Chaos, it wasn't to be.

To this day I can't quite believe that what happened did actually happen.

Some of the VIP guests that did make it never really understood what happened, and even if they read this, it won't get back the missed opportunity.

The shot at the hoop that missed by a mile can't be retaken. There aren't always "mulligans" in the real world.

Insights / Distinctions:

Is just having an intention enough? At some point, do we have to take the action steps to make forward progress toward our goals?

Joe Girard, an award-winning salesman, motivational speaker, and author certainly thought so and speaks to that in his saying, "The road to success is paved with good intentions, but they will never get you there. You have to take the steps."

If we believe this, and for a moment assume it to be the case, then the question becomes: what actions "should" I/someone/we take? What people really mean is, "What is likely to produce the outcomes I want without the negative outcomes I do not want to experience?"

Potentially, they consider, "What is the optimal action that will produce the outcomes I'm intending to create?"

Those are very simple yet very dense and complex questions to answer.

For almost all of our lives, we realise how little we can predict.

Buckminster Fuller highlighted precession which can be simply defined for now as the effect of bodies in motion on other bodies in motion

Precessionary side effects play a big part in this being the case, but in addition, most of our models of reality are flawed; our measurement of the relevant data is incomplete or inaccurate.

It's more than this, though: rarely do we acknowledge ourselves for our intentions and creating successfully super simple things. Our "failures" skew our experiences.

Even when we do create successfully then we can't have 100% certainty as to causality, as we've covered earlier, although often we believe we do have it.

I believe this is one of the traps we have created for ourselves as humans. We may have Clarity about an outcome we're looking to create. Yet we use our old "2D/linear" thinking and limit our thoughts about how it can be created.

I'm sure you've heard the phrase "out-of-the-box thinking"? Most ideas are simple rehashes of what's come before; most of the brilliance and magic of the world lives in the exploration and harnessing of our true creativity.

Let's look at intentions for a moment.

Intentions can be real and aligned, or they can be illusory. We believe that we or others have an intention. Yet when it is challenged, it dissolves like the morning mist. At other times, the intention shines bright and holds true and stands up to all manners of challenges for decades and even lifetimes.

Intentions can be logical and understood, or almost hard-wired and primal.

They can be singular, yet all too often they are jumbled, interlaced, and in conflict. We intend to do the "right thing" – to be on time, be healthy, connect with our friends, have a good time, be successful, make a difference, not work all the time.

How do we prioritise these and more? That's another chapter.

I also think that often we don't even really know why we have the intentions we have, and they are entangled and layered up. Some people suggest that really all our life is driven by genetic sequences: the intention to reproduce and propagate – as if we humans are simply puppets to our genetics. Psychology and other disciplines have libraries of ideas on why humans do what we do – to impress our parents or a potential mate; to not stand out and be removed from the tribe and thus maintain our chances of survival; to connect and not be alone.

Why do *you* think people do what they do?

Why do you?

For the last few years, with one of my super special Strategic Alchemy Lab partners, we have had a saying: "People are weird." It suggests that we love weird people, and that we ourselves are people and do weird things. It also allows a short cut when others or we ourselves start to wonder and ask why people have done something that to us makes no sense at all.

It's a modern trope: being triggered… dehydrated… low sugar… not enough sleep… they were drunk… As excuses for when people go, "oops, what was that about?" – when they weren't themselves.

I'd like you to consider:

- Can we have Clarity about our intentions and not outcomes?
- What about the other way around?
- Does the intention matter if the outcome is the same?

There's an old saying – the road to hell is paved with good intentions.

If a chef makes lunch, and the diner is poisoned because of an unknown allergy, surely it matters if the chef intended to or not?

Yet intentions are so hard to understand and so opaque in our modern world. Especially where unethical marketers have learnt to profile and press buttons, to cause a call and response. Many billions of pounds are regularly invested into "getting" people to buy things and act in ways that don't come naturally. When a stranger knocks on your door and interrupts your day to "just ask you a few questions", how many of us really have a neutral response? We've learnt really to distrust others' intentions – often because we know how *we* can be. Do you think this is wise? Optimal?

Our nursery rhymes and myths teach us to beware "Greeks bearing gifts", the wolf knocking at the door, and the poisoned apple. If someone assumes everything is as it seems at face value, then they are thought of as naïve.

I've been scammed more than I believed I could be, and I'm sure we all have had moments where we feel taken for granted; where we took people's intentions for granted. We're not stupid, right?

I also know that we're all human. We make mistakes, even with the best of intentions.

Have you ever set off to a meeting and been delayed, and arrived late or perhaps missed it completely? I know I have more than once (see above!).

What about losing track of time, not hearing an alarm, and missing a deadline that way?

Have you ever intended and really wanted to have a great conversation and build a personal or business relationship only for something you said to be misinterpreted and the whole thing blow up?

In fact, outcomes can happen often with no intention logically present to us at all.

When we go from theory to reality in a multi-human world, there must be something that can be gleaned to help us be with the Chaos.

In a competition, two sports teams both intend to win… yet only one can. It isn't possible for them to both achieve the outcomes they intend. Does the fan at home shouting at the TV really make a difference to the result? We often laugh at superstitions. Yet almost all professionals at the top of their game have some – especially those they don't believe to be superstitions.

It's more common than not for someone who intends to get healthy to exercise and then have an injury from that exercise that leaves them worse off than before they started. Does that mean the intentions were bad? I don't think so – it's just a reminder that we don't have mastery yet of ourselves and our world. There's Chaos that dances and laughs at our plans – at times with such vigour that it all seems to spite us with a vengeance our ancestors assigned to the old Gods.

Today, as I'm writing this book, it was time to pause and take care of myself and my health. One of my ongoing intentions. To this end, I considered my options. I intended to get a nice healthy sushi lunch. The weather was cold, yet as I walked the sun came out, and I found myself having some creative insights, including many of those I've included in this very chapter. These ideas you're reading now and many other small outcomes, including some exercise, resulted, which I never would have predicted when I set out.

Would it matter if, when I arrived, the restaurant was closed? For me in that walk and moment, it wouldn't. I had already experienced many good positive outcomes. Yet if I had known it was closed before I set off, I never would have walked that way, and maybe would have just stayed inside.

The good news (I think good news) is that the restaurant was open as I predicted and as it "should have been", and they had room at the bar where I could enjoy a seaweed salad and some green tea. If they hadn't had space, with the sun out I could have opted for a takeaway to eat in the park or at home or done many other different things – made easier by the fact that I have known this area for many years and have come up with multiple ways to create workability over the years. It was terrain and territory I knew. Does that alter my ability to respond in the moment?

Some people love to be a "stranger in a strange land" – to walk around unknown streets exploring. I do at times. Yet I've also found myself walking in a desert with no map and no one around for miles, all for taking the wrong turn at a river, assuming it would all work out. Thankfully it did, but the human body really doesn't do well in intense heat without water.

Here though I had the intention to eat sushi and without any drama created the outcome for myself (touch wood or, as we say, "God willing"). Simple, and I'm sure you can and do similar daily. This ability points to something. We can be very effective at creating outcomes from intentions at times. What makes the difference between it happening easily and it never happening?

The ancient Greeks and many others would remind people not to think it's all due to them in case, taken over by hubris (arrogance), they suffered nemesis (disaster).

In the Arabic world, "In sha'Allah", meaning "if God wills" or "God willing", follows almost every intention.

So how will you dance between the world of being able to create your reality and being intentional, and the world of being at the mercy of outcomes beyond your ken?

This is the exploration and inquiry that opens up when you consider intentions and outcomes.

Thought Experiment: The Paperclip Challenge:

Consider a simple paperclip.

Set yourself a timer and come up with as many things you could use it for as you can in, say, a minute.

Then set another timer and repeat the process.

How many of those have you actually done?

If you asked other people, how many of the ideas you came up with, would they also have thought of?

What if you asked everyone on Earth?

If coming up with a new use case would earn you one million pounds, would you be able to come up with some more ideas? Would you take different actions?

Where did you limit your thoughts about how to achieve the "goal" of coming up with as many uses as possible?

Be honest – did you consider asking other people? The internet? AI?

Did the time constraint play a part?

What if it would save the life of someone you cared about – what would change?

What if it would save *your* life?

What if it would save all our lives?

If you're doing that in this simple example, where else could you be limiting your own thinking and capabilities about achieving your outcomes?

Note: This is a thought experiment based on a live experience I had during one of the marketing mastery trainings over a decade ago with Alex Mandossian. I hope it gives you some greater Clarity and amazing insights now and into the future.

As the trainer's mentor Roy H. Williams told me live at his "Wizard's Academy", "Why did you get in the box in the first place?" (*in relation to limiting our thinking around questions and the need to try to think "outside the box")*.

The Key Questions:

- What are my intentions right now?
- Where did they come from?
- Are they serving me optimally?
- What impact do they have on you and your outcomes?
- Are they optimal for you?

Summary:

Here we've looked at the nature of intentions and outcomes, and how they have an interesting relationship that will transform as we ourselves transform and shift from Chaos to Clarity.

We've highlighted the importance of remembering to avoid hubris and be mindful of the ways things actually happen.

More than anything, we've started to explore how intentions and outcomes can lead to Chaos, even when we all agree the goal is Clarity.

Chapter 9

Choices, Commitments, and Consequences

> "You are free to make whatever choice you want, but you are not free from the consequences of the choice."
>
> — Unknown

For most people alive today there seems to be more choice than ever.

In life we make choices (and decisions) most of which we aren't fully conscious of. Sometimes they align with our commitments, and sometimes they seem in conflict.

The consequences of these choices and commitments aren't just immediate, and sometimes it's not until decades later that we get a glimpse perhaps of a road not travelled.

These choices we're free to make in theory, but how many of us are truly free?

Commitments seemingly keep us trapped but can also be the very structures to give us freedom and Clarity. Yet one person's courageous commitment is another person's insanity.

Consequences can seem predictable, but like much we've covered, thanks to the reality of Chaos can change on a dime, moment by moment.

In this chapter we'll explore the subjects of choices, commitments, and consequences and their correlations.

We'll also point at the opportunity to shift your perspective and approach to these subjects and in so doing give yourself greater possibility for Clarity.

Story: Never Surrender

I wanted to share with you this true story of the Japanese soldier Hiroo Onoda who was tasked with defending his post in the Second World War. He went far beyond what most people would think was "reasonable" as he continued to fight for nearly three decades after Japan's surrender.

Onoda was a young officer in the Imperial Japanese Army who was sent to the Philippines in 1944. He was stationed on the remote island of Lubang and given strict orders to never surrender, continue the fight, and gather intelligence.

When the war ended in 1945, Onoda and his small group of soldiers refused to believe the news, dismissing it as enemy propaganda. They continued their guerrilla activities, evading capture and living off the land.

Despite encountering leaflets and messages from locals urging them to surrender, Onoda and his comrades remained committed to their mission.

Over the years, attempts were made to locate and convince Onoda to surrender, but he remained steadfast. He held out day after day, month after month, year after year.

On 20 February 1974, Onoda met Norio Suzuki, a Japanese man who was traveling around the world looking for "Lieutenant Onoda, a panda, and the Abominable Snowman, in that order".

Suzuki found Onoda after four days of searching. Onoda described that moment in a 2010 interview: "This hippie boy Suzuki came to the island to listen to the feelings of a Japanese soldier. Suzuki asked me why I would not come out…"

Onoda and Suzuki became friends, but Onoda still refused to surrender, saying that he was waiting for orders from a superior officer. Suzuki returned to Japan with photographs of himself and Onoda as proof of their encounter, and the Japanese government located Onoda's commanding officer, Major Yoshimi Taniguchi, who had surrendered long ago and since become a bookseller.

Taniguchi went to Lubang Island, and on 9 March 1974, he finally met with Onoda and fulfilled a promise he had made back in 1944: "Whatever happens, we'll come back for you."

Taniguchi then issued Onoda the following orders:

1. In accordance with the Imperial command, the Fourteenth Area Army has ceased all combat activity.
2. In accordance with military Headquarters Command No. A-2003, the Special Squadron of Staff's Headquarters is relieved of all military duties.
3. Units and individuals under the command of Special Squadron are to cease military activities and operations immediately and place themselves under the command of the nearest superior officer. When no officer can be found, they are to communicate with the American or Philippine forces and follow their directives.

Onoda was thus properly relieved of duty, and he surrendered. He turned over his sword, a functioning Arisaka Type 99 rifle, 500 rounds of ammunition, and several hand grenades, as well as the dagger his mother had given him in 1944 to kill himself with if he was captured.

So, it was not until 1974, almost three decades after its end, that he was convinced that the war was indeed over.

This summary of a true story is I think worth considering for so many reasons.

- What would you have done in his position?
- Where do you have that level of commitment in your own life?
- Where could you?

Insights / Distinctions:

On a daily basis we take and are given opportunities to make a choice.

Some of these happen even as we wake. Will I get up now or try and sleep a little more? Will I make my bed or do that later? Will I check my phone now or later?

So many of these choices aren't really choices, and it's something that causes a lot of Chaos or confusion.

What is a choice?

It's actually quite hard to define.

What isn't a choice maybe clearer?

Do we really live at choice in our lives and in the world?

Did I choose my name, the language I think and speak, the culture and country I grew up in? Some would point at "spiritual beliefs" and "soul contracts" and say yes. However, I would suggest that for now in a grounded way, we don't.

We do get potentially to choose how we respond to these external stimuli. Choice or robotic automated response. Can we distinguish between reactions and responses?

Is a choice a choice if there are consequences we are scared of for ourselves or others – be those real fears or imagined?

Most people I've met in my life – and myself – have lived at some level from fear in our lives. We are trying to survive, to earn money to "pay the bills", to keep the respect and "love" of our people.

Children when young don't know the rules of the world, the written and unwritten laws, and will often behave in ways that surprise and embarrass their parents. It can be a source of joy or great frustration.

As adults we learn to conform (or some decide to not conform). There really isn't any other choice, right? You conform or you don't.

At school a teacher described as a choice an option between at least three things – X, Y, or Z. Most think a choice is just between A or B. Other training I've done has suggested that a choice is only a choice if there are no "reasons" for it other than that you chose it.

When we are "forced" to choose is it really a choice?

If you were asked to choose between A and B right now.. which would you chose?

Do you now notice how we ignore the full set of possible outcome choices?

We tend to discount or ignore or not even consider the options of both (A and B), neither (not A nor B), and definitely not the infinite other options.

You could argue this is just being normal and the way social conventions work. Being normal / average isn't really what this book is about and wants for you. Most people are not thriving or truly in love with their lives. This book is a stand for you having a major breakthrough.

So, let's continue.

A bit like possibilities, I find it fascinating that choices which seemingly are a part of our very essence are also for myself quite intangible and tricky to pin down.

When someone says, "Would you like a coffee or tea?", is there an auto-response or a real choice to say yes or no or both or something completely different?

How often in a restaurant or café would you choose to ask for something that isn't on the menu?

How can we ask for something we have never experienced or perhaps don't even know exists?

What's fascinating is how much we program ourselves – let alone allow others and the outer world to program us. Especially in the hyper-connected advertising and attention-grabbing modern technology world.

I look around often and wonder how I ended up doing and buying and experiencing most of what I have in my 45 years. Much arose not inside me naturally but from outer influences and suggestions.

When I looked up a definition of choice, this is what I found:

> Choice can be defined as the act or process of selecting or making a decision between two or more possibilities or options. It involves evaluating alternatives and making a conscious selection based on personal preferences, values, or circumstances.

This highlights that for many, choices and decisions are synonymous. Decisions, however, I don't think are choices. They may look like them from the outside, but metaphysically I would like you to try on just for now that they are distinct.

Decisions are about cutting off possibilities. The meaning of the word 'decide' comes from the Latin word *decidere*, which is a combination of two words: *de* = 'OFF' and *caedere* = 'CUT'. In the extreme I've heard it as "murdering possibilities". It's an unusual way to think about it, but also quite accurate.

When you decide, it's an affirmative action. This is a key aspect that ties to the idea of commitment. My experience of elite performers – in sports, business, and special forces groups – reinforces this. They understand the power of commitment and making the decision to do whatever it takes to achieve their goals. When commitment combines with capability, truly extraordinary results are possible.

One way to consider a real choice is to be standing on a great plain in good weather with no deadline in time and no location you have to get to, with more than enough food and water and shelter. Now which way will you go, or will you simply stay where you are? Have you ever had a stroll in the summer like this?

Did you choose your path? Did something pique your interest? Perhaps something inner called/caused you to take the steps you did?

Even the simple act of eating gives us space to explore the nature of choice. Consider your most recent meal that you enjoyed. Why did you enjoy it? Did you choose the things you ate? How much of that is a function of past associations or suggestions from culture/the marketplace?

It's interesting, I think, to notice how food preferences vary massively between cultures – not just spice levels, but also the textures and the approach to what is a delicacy and what is not on the menu at all.

As we alluded to above, for every choice taken or not taken, there are consequences.

In the arena of food, there is a clichéd quote, "A moment on the lips; an inch on the hips." This points to how quickly we move into decision, balancing our short term/long term desires, balancing the instant thirst for gratification with our commitments and desires. In nature, so much more seems to live in the moment, whereas in our world of complex interactions and financial pressures, we learn to play a more and more constricted game trying to maintain what we have or get what we haven't.

If you've ever studied – be it a new skill, a martial art, or a musical instrument – with any level of real commitment, you'll have had to face the paradox of short-term pleasure vs. long-term pain, or short-term pain vs. long-term pleasure.

I know personally that the hours invested with no obvious short-term result were driven by some level of commitment. What was it to, though?

We like to think it's because we have a clear why, but often the why isn't so clear. Perhaps we have a commitment to our perception of how we should be. We are committed to getting a goal we've created for ourselves, or to avoid a punishment/negative experience – be it externally or internally created.

Even more fascinating are those times when we have a moment of "not thinking", when we say to ourselves or others, "trust me". In those moments did we really choose? Sometimes they work out and sometimes they don't. Either way, is it a wise approach you'd want to use as a primary strategy?

Decision Theory is a branch of mathematics that focuses on analysing and making "rational decisions" in situations involving uncertainty and multiple possible outcomes. It encompasses various subfields, such as Game Theory, Probability Theory, Utility Theory, and Risk Analysis.

Together, these fields provide mathematical frameworks for understanding choices, commitments, and the consequences that arise from decision-making processes, allowing individuals and entities to make informed and rational decisions in complex and uncertain situations.

What's interesting to highlight is that "rational" is very much dependent on individual perspectives and biases. What may be considered rational for one person may differ from another based on their unique circumstances and perspectives.

In life and business, the consequences of making choices and decisions are not fair and balanced. The media will often encourage people to believe in going for it, yet when things go wrong the negative consequences may be catastrophic.

Risk and reward truly make life "interesting".

Your ability to be informed and intelligent will make all the difference.

In my own life, I've done the "right" thing more than once only for it to have significant negative consequences. When this happens, regrets build. Comparison is rarely useful, but it's human nature to look at what others have done and think, "if only I had (or hadn't) made the choices I did."

If you find yourself full of regret or fear about making choices, then I would recommend you seek professional help to give you different perspectives. This can be in many forms, from a counsellor to a business advisor. Equally, remember that we are all human, and as you'll see in the bonus story at the end of this chapter, we never know what the future will hold. Regret and feeling like a victim can be very disempowering. Yet so much of the reality of Chaos is outside of our control. We will all lose people in our lives that we care about. The world isn't yet an infinite endless utopia, and I doubt we'll get there any time soon. Grieving what could have been and giving ourselves time and space to "miqui" the past takes courage and work.

Miqui is a term I love that comes from my study with Terry Stout and has its roots in the wisdom of the Inka and the Chakana. It refers to letting nature naturally process the past, removing what is toxic and leaving good nutrients for the future.

A distinction that I'd like to share and that can be empowering to own your choices is "I could be, and I CHOOSE not to be." This allows you to acknowledge that you have options and be in the driving seat of your life, not acting as a victim or passenger.

If and when we start with nothing and from nothing, we have a simpler choice really to move forward. As you invest time and energy and money into your endeavours, you build structures external and internal that make some choices easy and others seemingly impossible.

Today would you risk everything you have to start a new life with no guarantees of what consequences will come? I know that I wouldn't. I'm grateful for the lessons I've learnt and proud of what I've built.

As you get clearer about what risks you face and could face, and your capacity and willingness to engage and respond to them, you will be able to step more into the possibility of Clarity in relation to your choices.

In the limit, there is the possibility of being ok with who you are and without need to prove or get anywhere. As a result, you could choose moment by moment and navigate with the fun and joy that I imagine a wild dolphin has as they dance in the surf on a summer's day.

I've been in this flow at times, and it's extraordinary. At other moments I've jammed myself into train and tube carriages day after day full of hot sweaty people looking miserable, because my younger self believed, "I didn't have a choice.".

As I write this, the truth is that I didn't really understand my choices and I'm still getting clear as to what's possible and what was for myself back then.

I do believe that you won't even consider the choice or decision for something that you don't think is possible. Just as in a restaurant when presented with a menu, few people will consider and ask for things that aren't on the menu at all.

When we consider not just our own individual choices and commitments and consequences, but how they occur in our various collective groups, the subject devolves more and more to apparent Chaos. Yet even within the Chaos there is room for Clarity – or perhaps the possibility of Clarity at the boundaries.

I'm writing this today on planet Earth. Am I choosing to be on this planet, or do I just find myself here? A few humans it seems in the last hundred years have gone off-planet, and at one time I even had a reserved place for a space shuttle seat. Will I ever fly off-planet? Perhaps. Is it my highest commitment? Not right now. Yet for many it's a burning passion that has them invest their lives and billions of pounds in exploring.

Equally if tomorrow a friendly advanced spaceship captain invited me to go on a quick journey – safely – I'd probably almost certainly says yes. Can I choose to make that happen?

All too many people get trapped in the mental trap of cause and effect, correlation and causation, and mechanics vs. manifestation.

Your invitation from this chapter is to start to be someone with greater certainty and Clarity about how you choose and what you commit to, and to navigate the consequences.

P.S. Love and a deeper distinction of decisions vs choices

When I shared this book with my dear friend Terry Stout, MsD he asked me to add this to help give an insight that he believes is vital if we are really to access Choice and Clarity successfully.

We have highlighted that choices are distinct from decisions. What we haven't distinguished optimally yet for a reader is whether it was a separate activity of the subjective mind or of the higher consciousness of the heart.

Most people don't even know there is such a distinction.

Decisions are made from a mind based Subjective Consciousness reasoning process, which is usually outer referenced and often fear based.

True Choices, on the other hand, arise from a much higher Heart Consciousness, which is based on non-verbal, "feeling" intelligence that is a conduit or portal between the lower and higher forms of consciousness or "Selves".

Choices, therefore, are usually (being of the Heart) based in Love.

Thought Experiments:

Journey

Imagine a journey – either a physical one or a life/business internal one.

If it's 20 years from now and you never got to reach the destination of your journey, would you still go on that journey?

If you made a commitment to do whatever it takes to complete the journey, when would you give up, if ever?

Just Ask

You are doing a training exercise on commitment. The context is set for the exercise that a code is essential to stop a bomb going off and killing everyone you care about (or perhaps you'd rather win a prize).

Your partner in the exercise opens an envelope with the instructions and the special code. You open your envelope, and it says, "Just ask for the code, and the exercise isn't completed until you have it."

So, what would you do?

If you asked for the code, and they say "no", then what would you do?

How would you feel? It's just a training exercise after all; would you laugh or get frustrated?

Would you ask again? What if they said "no" again?

How would you feel?

What would you do now?

Would you give up?

Want to know the twist? Ready to give up now?

Only read on when you're ready for the surprise…

You see that the instructions for your partner say, "Just say no, until they've asked you politely for the code ten times."

Would you have asked politely ten times?

Does that seem too easy?

What if you tried this with one of your friends, would they keep going?

P.S. I have actually done exercises like this a few times in the real world with different rules. It was very confronting and insightful, and yes frustrating and even amusing, as we watched all the ways we and other people "tried" to get the code and forgot to do what was suggested and "just ask".

The Key Questions:

- What am I choosing right now?
- How do I know?
- What am I choosing not to do right now?
- How do I know?
- What am I committed to?
- How do I know?
- Am I committed to responding to whatever the consequences are?
- What consequences could I plan ahead to handle?

Summary:

Commitment is something which lives in the metaphysical realm, and when I'm working with clients it can be a great access to Clarity for me and for them. Often what's crystal clear for an observer around our commitments is invisible in our blind spots or hidden from our conscious thoughts by ourselves.

When we remember what really matters, we can reflect and reset and align our commitments so that they create an inner and outer structure that's more and more optimal.

With the north star of what really matters shining bright, we can better navigate the circumstances that arise – those predicted and those unexpected – with a different attitude and make choices that support our direction and momentum more easily and effectively.

We could have started with these subjects, yet too often they take over and are used to whitewash the Chaos in the world and in people's minds.

Give yourself permission and time to really enquire into your commitments and choices, and their consequences.

As you go to sleep each day, no matter what you've done or not done, choose to reflect on what has come before, and know that as you wake in the morning your past does not define you.

Our lives are built moment by moment, choice by choice, commitment by commitment.

Complete the loops and new openings will arise.

It's said that "You never truly know the outcome of the movie of your life until you reach the very last frame."

Perhaps life's greatest plot twists remain hidden until the closing credits have rolled, revealing the unexpected climax of our own cinematic journey.

In our connected world, we may never truly know the consequences of our choices in our lifetime, and perhaps that's ok. All we can do is our best in each moment.

> "Until one is committed, there is hesitancy, the chance to draw back, always ineffectiveness. Concerning all acts of initiative and creation, there is one elementary truth the ignorance of which kills countless ideas and splendid plans: that the moment one definitely commits oneself, then providence moves too.
>
> "All sorts of things occur to help one that would never otherwise have occurred. A whole stream of events

issues from the decision, raising in one's favour all manner of unforeseen incidents, meetings, and material assistance which no man could have dreamed would have come his way.

"I have learned a deep respect for one of Goethe's couplets: Whatever you can do or dream you can, begin it. Boldness has genius, power, and magic in it. Begin it now."

— William Hutchison Murray

Bonus Story: The Chinese Farmer's Wisdom

Once upon a time, there was a Chinese farmer who lived with his son in a rural village. They had a small plot of land and a single horse that they used for farming. One day, the horse escaped from its stable and ran away.

The local villagers came to the farmer and expressed their sympathy, saying, "What a terrible misfortune! You've lost your horse. How will you work on the farm now? How will you survive? Whatever will you do?" However, the farmer replied calmly, "Good or bad, who knows?"

A few days later, the horse returned to the farm, accompanied by several wild horses. The villagers saw this and exclaimed, "What great luck! Now you have so many horses. You are very fortunate!" Once again, the farmer responded, "Good or bad, who knows?"

While trying to tame one of the wild horses, the farmer's son fell off and broke his leg. The villagers gathered around and said, "How unfortunate! Your son has been injured, and now he cannot help you with the farm work." The farmer's response remained the same: "Good or bad, who knows?"

Shortly after, the village received news of a war that had broken out. Soldiers from the emperor's army arrived in the village to enlist men in good health and sound bodies to fight. Due to his broken leg, the farmer's son was deemed unfit for the army. The villagers came to the farmer, expressing relief and saying, "What luck! Your son's injury saved him from going to war." And once again, the farmer replied, "Good or bad, who knows?"

The story of the Chinese farmer reminds us that what may initially seem like a misfortune can turn out to be a blessing, and vice versa. How we choose to perceive, react, and respond to circumstances is usually a function of our judgement of them.

Chapter 10

What Really Matters to You?

"The most important thing in life is to find out what is the most important thing."

— Shunryu Suzuki, Sōtō Zen Monk

There's what happens in reality. Then there is our perception of our "limited" observation of what actually happens. Then there is our actual reaction or response to our perception. Then there is our perception of our "limited observation" of our actual reaction or response to our perception.

While this may be accurate, it's not exactly super simple and fully understandable. More importantly how does this apply to you right now?

Right now, I'd like to propose that you have an opportunity to "try on" the idea that you can step into the frame of "Being 100% responsible – able to respond – to everything that does and does not happen". This is **Rule Three**.

Out of all there is that you can be responsible for, it makes sense to focus on what really matters.

What do we mean by "matters"?

This question has been there in the background for the whole duration of the book, and now it's time to unpack it.

One way "matters" can be defined is as someone or something being important or significant.

This is a subjective perception. Often as I thought about what to write and share, my mind conflated matters with "meaningful". They do have a similar quality yet are quite distinct ideas. I think many people often do the same.

I think it's also worth highlighting how what really matters is situational and contextual.

Inside a specific "game" or "goal" as scenarios play out, it may even be objective what matters and with a general consensus. Yet generally it's a function of perception, models, and paradigms.

In my audit and banking days, a lot of focus was put on the subject of something being "material". What is material again depends on the context and circumstances.

A £0.01 error in a bank balance for example. Would you consider that material?

It's just one penny after all, and most people would think it isn't. However, that error may highlight a system breakdown, a fraud, a breach of a regulation or law. Without the context, it can't be declared material or not. It's one of the reasons why auditors provide opinions not statements.

I saw this especially when working at Morgan Stanley in Product Control with credit derivatives and structured trades – where a seemingly immaterial (meaning not material) cash or profit and loss error could easily have been ignored when in fact it was a misbooking of a buy as a sell transaction.

The small errors in the moment, if not caught, can potentially create massive and catastrophic consequences down the line and years later.

Another good physical example is that of being one second out of time.

If you're one second early for the last call to catch a flight, it's probably immaterial and all good.

If you're one second late after the last call to catch a flight, it would be material and the flight would be gone without you.

A commonly shared example of this is the one-degree change, which on a projectile going a few centimetres makes hardly any material change. However, when your target is hundreds of miles away – the moon, say – that one-degree variation in orientation can mean that you miss your target by miles.

At times, I've asked you to consider the macro priorities and North Star for your life during this book – your underlying and overarching "what really matters".

These can help you consider what's material and what matters. However, it's often not until years or decades later that we can see what would (or wouldn't) have made the difference.

I personally experienced how those chance meetings or seemingly irrelevant choices often had profound consequences years later. On the good days you see how it all works out. On the bad days you may have regrets.

What you can have in this moment is a greater appreciation for the "game of life" and the choices you have as to where you direct your focus and draw your line of what matters.

The new skills and greater Clarity you've gained from reading this book can be applied to each and every domain and scale of life and business.

I think it's worth sharing a "P.S." at this point:

Sometimes the things we think are our biggest "breakdowns" can become our biggest "breakthroughs".

The movie and story are not over until they are over. All we can do is be in each moment as present and centred and optimal as we can.

Part of what makes this so complicated to be absolutely certain about – aside from the Chaos of the universe – is the nature and interaction of precessional, compounding or unexpected effects.

If we don't know the destination… and where we are… then how can we ever get there? Or know we're there when we arrive?

Lewis Carroll, in his famous novel *Alice's Adventures in Wonderland*, shared this idea in this dialogue between Alice and the Cheshire Cat:

> "Would you tell me, please, which way I ought to go from here?"
>
> "That depends a good deal on where you want to get to," said the Cat.
>
> "I don't much care where –" said Alice.
>
> "Then it doesn't matter which way you go," said the Cat.
>
> "– so long as I get SOMEWHERE," Alice added as an explanation.
>
> "Oh, you're sure to do that," said the Cat, "if you only walk long enough."

I think at times we act both as Alice and the Cat ourselves.

Rule Three is worth remembering here.

You get to be responsible whether you choose to set the destination or not for your journey in life in the world.

You will have choices and decisions to make – some that will be obvious and many that will slide by seemingly not there for the making. Their consequences and ripples are hardly ever known in reality before or even as we take them.

If we don't know what really matters… then what's the point?

We could have started here, but if we had, I think what you would have thought and realised would have been very different from what I think you'll see now.

Here with all the insights, tools, and distinctions we've built up, we'll look at what really matters.

Perhaps you've already got that Clarity as you've read through the book so far.

Either way, we'll explore next a way you can get clearer on what that is now.

As we continue to clear away some more false assumptions, you may notice a feeling arising, or the possibility of a feeling of clarity and certainty that is distinct. Like when someone finally gets the right prescription for their glasses, and actually has the glasses cleaned for the first time in their lives. Be open to these observations, and notice when you notice them.

Story: Richest Man In The World

Warning / Disclaimer – Read This Story Only If You Are of Sound Mind & Body:

One of my mentors/business partners and friends told me a version of this story and took me through this exercise in the office I had in Rotherhithe in my early 30s. It stuck with me, and it's quite confronting and unsettling. In the last few years, I personally experienced a few hemiplegic migraines, and these truly scary painful moments make sharing this all the more essential. If this story triggers you, then please reach out to someone you trust and talk about it – and if need be, your relevant local medical/mental health professional.

Remember, Being the Richest Man in the Graveyard Is Not Your Job

For many of us we have at times fantasised about wanting to be "The Richest Man/Woman in the World".

Whether you can admit to yourself that you have or not, I want you to imagine that you have made it and you are that person.

For not the first time, you're waking up in your ideal home, with the most amazing comfortable bedding and furniture.

There is beautiful artwork on the walls. The property is one of your properties, and it's a place you love and couldn't be better. It's been customised to your taste and fits you like a glove. You feel super secure and safe and happy here.

As you have come to expect, you have ready for you the most refreshing nourishing food and drink, and it's amazing to enjoy every bite and sip. Life is good. Life is great.

As you look out of the window, you're relaxed and happy and content. It's a beautiful day, and the scenery you see is beautiful and warms your soul.

When you're ready to, you see people that you respect and care about smiling back at you. You also see your vehicles polished and prepared ready to take you anywhere you like – you can drive/pilot them yourself of have a chauffeur do that while you relax.

Your body is feeling at ease and healthy, strong, and alive.

You pause and smile, thinking about the amazing things you're looking forward to doing.

Then you notice that you're on the floor, and there is a red mark that's getting bigger and bigger. Then you realise that it's your blood. You can't move. You can't speak. The mark is becoming a pool of blood. You feel life drifting away.

There is nothing you can do.

There is no help coming.

There is nothing else you can make happen.

This is the end.

Insights / Distinctions:

In an infinite universe you are never going to see, experience, or do everything in a finite time.

Now more than ever– with billions of people online – there are more profiles, comments, books, videos, and ideas than you could ever engage with deeply in a hundred lifetimes.

Be with that for a moment, the true enormity of the "infinite" task list, if that was what mattered – to see and do it all. I don't think or propose it is.

Your path to Clarity of what really matters to you out of the Chaos is not an algorithmic sequence you can follow. There is no guaranteed blueprint, so that when at point A you do X to get to point B.

Have you ever seen two people arguing the toss over something that served no purpose, no value, and you were clear from your perspective they were playing a lose-lose-lose game. Wasting time and energy?

Maybe you've invested hours trying to do something before realising it was never going to work out that way at all.

A tragic example I've seen play out all too often in the real world is people in the car park at an Ikea store trying to force giant boxes into a tiny car. In those moments all logic and reason go out of the window. Anyone can see they are never going to fit except for the people trying to squeeze them in before they hear the crack of wood or the shattering of glass. Even more fascinating when usually Ikea will deliver the furniture or delivery van services are often available.

Have you ever obsessed about getting something for days and weeks, only to receive it and be like, "Is that it"? Once must have toys or clothing sitting in a cupboard or attic forgotten.

In general, does it matter what anyone else was thinking about five years ago?

I would have you consider that almost all of what happens doesn't really matter. It's like moving grains of sand around a beach making sandcastles, only for it to be washed away by the next wave.

I am not a nihilist (a person who believes that life is meaningless). Far from it. I'm clear there are experiences that for me have given me tangible visceral experiences of meaning. I've also discovered that I play a part in those, and the things we've explored in this book make them more likely, not less.

There are times – like during a dark winter's night, when the weather is howling a gale – that all there is to do is take one breath at a time. The dawn will come. The reality of Chaos is like the surfer out at sea during a big swell: at times you will get knocked off your centre and feel at the mercy of the Chaos/of the world and wonder which way is up. This too shall pass.

Then there are those moments when you are in a state of grace and flow, and things happen with and for you more than you ever dreamt possible. When suddenly the Rubik's cube of life turns, and you see how the dots might connect in ways more beautiful and magical than you ever believed possible.

To someone who loves music, they can hear the melody, the harmony, and the genius in great songs. To someone without those distinctions, all they notice is noise.

Notes declaring "C = I x E" or "$E = MC^2$" would seem potentially random scribblings of a mad man to some, and to others a stroke of genius.

Perhaps beauty and meaning really is in the eye of the beholder.

You get to direct the camera lens of your life. You get to set the sail and the direction and timings of your tacking. As Buckminster Fuller imagined and stood for – you really do get to set the trimtab for your life, and perhaps the world, if you choose.

When I set out to the write this book, I had an intention and ideas of outcomes in mind. Yet the journey of writing the book has already shaped me more than I imagined at the outset. I'm present to that as I type these words on the laptop. Does it matter if this book is ever actually published or read? Yes, it might be nice.

An ego would say, "Oh yes… my book has to matter, and get out there and get all the awards." I've chosen as much as possible to be with the fact that I really don't think that "my" stuff matters to anyone. For me truly what really matters isn't about me and my life as I write this – it's you and making a difference and ideally helping play a part in making the difference to you.

My mother is a big piece of why I can think this way today. I've watched over my whole life who she has built herself into and how she has "gardened" her life while at the same time being there for others – both in her role as a doctor and far more in the way she trained herself to be with people. Her model of empathy and caring for patients helped me see that in others and discover more than I ever dreamt possible. I've also grown up watching how she has been impacted by the paralysis caused by the poliovirus, and more how others often ignore of don't consider other people at all. It's also been a real reminder of the simple things that matter that others take for granted.

Doing the right thing isn't always popular or celebrated or acknowledged.

As I re-read these words today, I'm being with that. It doesn't make it easier. Being right some would say can be its own reward. I'm not sure that being "right" is enough or will be in the world as it is today.

The "goal of life" isn't for me about being the most popular, the most liked. Does it really matter who had the most downloads on a streaming service twenty years ago? Or who got the most likes on the social media reels last week?

You may say "Yes… it does".

Then great, you have your Clarity about what really matters to you and can act accordingly.

Memento mori (Latin for 'remember that you have to die') is a statement that most of humanity buys into. As I promised earlier, for this book I'm going to keep in the normal grounded mechanical world, so let's not explore for now whether that too is just an assumption.

Memento Mori is worth bringing to our attention at this point, as it's something I know that I generally have been unaware of or deliberately tried to avoid being with for most of my life – while simultaneously being almost hyper-aware at times of the fragility of human life, human beings, and my own well-being.

In the Western world, most people you meet will not have thought about their death in a grounded way. More and more we hide from this part of the natural cycle. We live as if we have infinite childlike "Peter Pan" lives. In fact, the idea of being able to live forever young as Peter did is so appealing, it's a common trope in modern music, film, and media.

So perhaps that's not the path to our "happily ever after" end credits.

It's at this point that we can touch on some of the ideas of Cathedral Thinking and beyond. This is where you allow your focus to be on long-term projects or goals realised for the sake of or for the benefit of future generations. Often these projects would not be completed in a single lifetime, and the people working on them may never see them completed.

Finding your path between this moment, your life, and your legacy in a way that is congruent to you is part of the journey of your life and this world that I've called "The World Quest™".

Different schools of philosophy, cultures, and religions will offer you their approach and rationality. In truth, I believe more and more that you get to create your rules for living. You get to declare what really matters to you.

You don't have to explain and validate it to anyone else.

There is nothing you have to prove to anyone in this world, in relation to your own internal declaration of value and utility (usefulness) and meaning.

You may want and need to with integrity find a way to communicate, collaborate and create with others. You may even choose to compromise to do so. It's possible to do this with love and joy. Yet few I've experienced actually will.

I also believe that too often today people are allowed to go off the track and, in many ways, robotically oscillate between convention and being rebels – while all the while never really doing the work to get to the core of what really matters to themselves.

In the ontology world, there is a paradox around the freedom of being, where with all the infinite possibilities we are still constrained to be like our mother/father or not like our mother/father.

As I stated at the beginning of this book, I'm not going to tell you that what really matters is x, y or z.

Even if I could I don't think you'd believe me, or it would serve you optimally.

I think each day and each moment you get a chance to observe, internalise, and then externalise your world view of meaning.

Human beings seem to be great at discerning and generating meaning.

Individually and collectively, we have more chance than ever to connect and communicate, and even perhaps engage in real collaboration. In that process, new information, insight, and perspective are made available to add into the alchemical melting pots of our lives.

Out of this, if you choose to you – and especially if you've been actively reading along in this book – you can be more equipped than ever to Pause… Stop… and Reflect… before you Reset towards what really matters to you.

I have some good and some bad news; which would you like first?

Isn't it interesting how we still have our judgements and preferences about these simple things.

The bad news is that sometimes you will not know what really matters until it's too late. We can't always turn back the clock and go again. You can't unburn the burnt toast. We all will lose things and people we love and care about, and not always at a time and in a way that seems fair.

Yet don't fear this. Be with the nature of Chaos as you have been more and more in this book and in your life.

The good news is that tomorrow is a brand-new day. A full 86,400 seconds during which anything is possible. You have more power to shift your focus into what really matters than many dream possible. Your inner world is your domain.

Your external circumstances today and whatever you have scheduled to do and end up doing, is just what it is. Like the stonemasons we talked about earlier in the book, your focus on what really matters to you can transcend all those things.

Thought Experiments:

Let's play a game

Imagine you're playing a simple "pointless" computer game with someone you care about and respect deeply. If you're stuck to think of one, perhaps tic-tac-toe/noughts and crosses.

When you stop playing the game and go back to "the real world", would it really matter who had won that particular game?

Would your caring and respect be altered by it?

If so, why?

If not, why not?

PGC

PGC stands for Pre-Galileo Complex. Before Galileo, the world thought the Earth – our planet – was the centre of the universe.

What is the centre of the universe? Of your universe? Do you think it's you?

Moving Pebbles Nowhere

Imagine if every day you went outside and selected three pebbles, and then slowly with full presence moved them a few feet, one by one.

Then slowly with full presence moved them back again, one by one.

Not random pebbles, but pebbles that you choose.

You get to say where you move them to.

You get to choose how long it takes, and when you do it.

If the pebbles are back where they started, what matters about the process?

What do you expect you would notice?

If you were being paid to this, would it alter your experience?

What if you were being forced to this, then would it alter your experience?

The Key Questions:

- What does it mean for something to matter?
- What doesn't matter?
- What do I care about?
- If there was a fire, what would I want to save?
- What would I give up everything for?
- What would I do everything to accomplish?

Summary:

How are you doing right now?

How are you feeling?

We've covered a lot in this book in a short time and in a few short pages. I've done my best to condense decades of exploration and inquiry, insights, and ideas in a way that will give you the best chance possible to shift from Chaos To Clarity™.

Perhaps you've started to *grok* something – know something with a Clarity and certainty that is different now for you than it was before. Maybe it's something you've glimpsed before, and maybe it's surprising you as it unfolds.

When we started this journey of the book together, neither of us knew exactly what the results would be, and even as we come to near the end of this book, we still don't. Often, I've found it's not till decades later when the dots connect that we see the magical paths we weaved through life.

I'd love you to reflect and journal and share openly what you got from reading this book with the people you care about, with the world, and with me.

I meant what I wrote… I really care about people and making the difference.

While I'm here on planet Earth, I want to find a way to be useful, valuable, creative, real, and alive. I'm beyond grateful to so many people, I couldn't name them all in a hundred books, and many of whom I don't even know their names. The people who did the things that mattered in the moments while the world was asleep, while no one was watching, and never got the fanfares and awards and global celebrations.

I know this – you matter.

What really matters to you doesn't exist in pages and theory but lived in the world, and as you take each breath and live each day, you now have the tools and opportunity to increase your Clarity about it until it's so bright and clear that it can help you navigate the most challenging time and inspire those who glimpse it from afar.

It's a privilege to share with you in this book, and I can't wait to see who you will become and what you will create as you remember more and more what really matters to you.

Chapter 11

Closing Note | A Personal Reflection on Chaos

"We walk in the shadows not of the dark."

— LSH

Each and every time when I forget it's there, the universe seems to relish in the surprising reminder of its immense capacity for Chaos.

I have had moments, more than once, of which I am very grateful, where I wake up and the world feels calm, beautiful and at ease. Where I believe and "know" I have time and space and nothing that I need to do.

I have also had moments, more than once, where I wake up and the world is seemingly ok and yet there is a feeling that something is "off", or worse something is "wrong".

In some way the contrast between these moments is what makes it possible to cause and create and gives us the distinctions to build and grow.

Perhaps you've had these moments, or perhaps you haven't yet.

However, from my research over decades, I think they represent a key element of the human condition – well at least as we are now – of our understanding, integration, evolution, and perhaps in time transformation.

It seems, given our model of evolution, that at some point we were not the meaning making machines we seem to have become and operated more in a wild primal state. Far into the future perhaps we'll evolve into beings of light fully aligned with this universe we find ourselves in. For now though, and I sense for the foreseeable future, the human condition will be much as it is now.

When you wake up and you know you're super cold or super hungry or super thirsty, it's easy for the body and brain to be focused into the "clear" urgent priority.

I remember waking up during a hike and camping trip and opening the zip of the tent to be surprised by the sight of nearly a foot of snow. I had seen snow many times before in my life, but it wasn't forecast, and I never expected it – not there and not then. We didn't have the clothing or preparations to handle it, but that's what we had to deal with. We didn't have a backup, and this was before the world of mobile phones and near instant taxis and deliveries.

Buckminster Fuller used to reference one of The Key Questions, "What's the most important thing we can be thinking about right now?"

In the moments of pressing physical need, we gain a sense of something.

Is it Clarity or something else? An innate drive to survive? A hardwired prioritisation?

At times I can remind myself, know, and experience intellectually that our present experience is a complex dance of functional interpretations of our perceptions of the past and our predictions of our expected futures.

Yet those primal priorities win over and have a quality that is profoundly distinct to most of our living moments.

In youth we are innocent to the grinds of time – the sways of the body and mind through the waves of business and personal relationships, and the almost infinite depths and currents of our own inner worlds.

For me, the enquiry of how to learn to sit comfortably in the moments of Chaos isn't just intellectual. It has become an undercurrent of focus for over twenty years.

At the simplest, this inquiry can be rephrased as, "How to get out of your own way and remember what really matters".

I have learnt much and clearly have even more to learn, integrate, and master.

There have been moments when you're facing dark nights of the soul, when nothing makes sense and seemingly Chaos has won the day. Those moments when often we seem powerless at the effect of the world. They are humbling.

Almost every entrepreneur I know has gone through these moments – and often when they least wanted to. Do they get easier? I'm not sure they do. We can learn to recognise them, perhaps. I don't think as you learn to feel more and be more it gets any easier.

This is because I do believe that when we remove the confusion of our minds and perceptions, we do at some level have a real sense of what matters.

Some might have you consider that nothing really matters, yet I can't believe that to be true. I choose not to believe it.

There is a full-body visceral reaction that I've come to call home. I just wish I would wake up there and be there at all times. That perhaps is the journey of enlightenment, of mastery.

Whenever we think we have it handled, another level reveals itself, or perhaps the basics must be practised and lived each day. The master surfer can still slip and fall off a simple small wave. The tai chi master can still be pushed by the beginner's push. On the good days, we laugh.

I have come to understand that fighting and hating the Chaos isn't wise or helpful. Yes, for many years my inner child had a primal scream at the unfairness of events beyond my control that destroyed the happy world that could have been. It wasn't fair that my mother suffered the way she did as a young girl at the hands of polio. What she went through was a catalyst that helped her become an amazing doctor and trainer of doctors. In turn it played a major part in shaping me via her. The ripples carry on.

I'm holding stuff back as I write this as some of the emotions are still so strong and real. Others' stories are theirs to tell. It's an honour and privilege for me to be a space for people to share and support them as they deal with the Chaos in their lives – health, business, personal, and more globally. It never gets easier. Not for me. I care about people massively. I've learnt to put on the auditor's/accountant's/ consultant's listening mode. Inside I feel a lot and wish I could click my fingers and make things right.

Yet, as we've explored, Chaos is the very nature of our world and has been since day one.

What I can say and would want you to know – just as if you were my dear friend and dealing with challenges – is that you are not alone.

You are amazing. More so than you realise and not for the reasons you might think.

You are human, and you have more strength and capacity than you imagine.

Your biggest disasters can be your biggest learnings and help you become stronger than you ever dared to dream might be possible and in ways you would never understand in advance.

This doesn't make them "right" or "fair", or easy to accept.

As you learn to master and integrate the distinctions and inquiries, I've shared in this book I believe you'll become better at understanding others and helping them in their journey too.

My wish is that through this work of "Chaos To Clarity", we might all find a way to come home and remember what really matters, and to do so before it's too late and we must live with our regrets.

Together I hope that while there is still time, one day we really can be more than enough. A world where everyone has enough water, food, and shelter. No one has to suffer from wounds that can be healed. No one suffers needless fear. A world of creativity and integrity and real collaboration.

No one is enslaved, used, and thrown away. No one left behind.

I've seen that world and lived it in my mind for many decades.

Wouldn't that be amazing?

Can you imagine your Eden?

An optimal "Eden" is great in theory.

However, we have to learn to be with reality, to clean up our past and our old behaviours and be really ready to step into a brighter future. That journey includes for each person understanding not only our own questions and answers but other people's too.

Do you remember the question we started with – which I hope now you understand differently:

"**Do I know what really matters to me now?**"

Chapter 12

Next Steps and New Openings for Action

> "The only way to do great work is to love what you do. If you haven't found it yet, keep looking. Don't settle. As with all matters of the heart, you'll know when you find it."
>
> — Steve Jobs

Now we're at the stage where we've ended the book, and you get to look ahead.

As Winston Churchill famously said, "Now this is not the end. It is not even the beginning of the end. But it is, perhaps, the end of the beginning."

My goal here in this chapter is to set you up for greater success in whatever you choose to focus on.

Are you familiar with this saying?

> "Before enlightenment there is chop wood, carry water.
> After enlightenment there is chop wood, carry water."

I truly believe – as my friend Terry keeps reminding me – that as you come "home" to who you really are. Not your own or the world's limited view of you but who you really are, that you will naturally start to remember what really matters.

Even if – and especially if – you don't believe you ever knew.

The experience of the discovery and exploration of clarity in the real world is far distinct from any story or hear say about it.

This remembering may come to you in a sudden "download", in a gentle unfolding process, or it may happen in a way that completely surprises you.

You never know when something will spark a connection, when something that's been invisibly blocking may "miqui" and dissolve, and then there it is an area of clarity you never imagined possible.

Have you ever walked in nature and become lost? You lose the path which seems to dissolve away into the wild. As you keep going, you eventually re-find a path. Perhaps intuition, perhaps a sign you notice, and then in time you find yourself back on a well-trodden path.

So it is with the living with these distinctions.

Each day you'll be either in a great place with clarity or discover you have fallen back into Chaos. In these moments you now have new choices to navigate.

You may even learn to love the chaos like a masterful windsurfer who enjoys the big waves and winds.

I also believe that you can build structures – physical, electronic, and metaphysical – which you can lean on when you need to. For me this includes both physical spaces, physical activities, and real relationships and agreements with trusted people and partners.

One of my inner circle people clients and partners calls this pedalling – moving between the inner "magic" and the external "mechanics" on a regular basis.

So now I'd like permission to ask you a question…

Are you ready – in a way that's safe for you – for you to get out of your own way fully now and remember what really matters?

I hope so.

Listen to your inner voice. Sometimes we have been hurt in the past, and have concerns about stepping out again, This is natural.

If you found yourself saying, "not now". Know that that is ok.

They say, **"Awareness is the first point of change."**

It's a journey and we all take steps as best we can.

I have a belief that your full potential wants to be revealed. I believe you stepping into your masterful ability to be in and with Clarity is part of that.

The ancient Greeks talked about this as "entelechy". Other communities throughout history have their versions of this.

What if this was true? Let's just try this on for a moment or two.

They say the universe gives you the lesson you need next – not necessarily the one you want. When things show up and occur perhaps they are opportunities for you to upgrade and gain more clarity. Sometimes trying on this perspective can help you find the value in each moment and experience.

I don't believe you picked up this book and read as far as you did "by chance". It has been designed and architected to help people who are ready for it. Gems of genius hidden inside to be uncovered and revealed and to empower people on their journeys in life. There is also space for "chance" and synchronous beneficial experiences to arise.

I know for sure that I have written it with an intent as I've disclosed several times – to Make The Difference. As I write this and as you read these words, know that I remain a stand for synchronicities that make the difference for my clients, friends and now for you. I always was if truth be told, but now you know me a little and it seems fair to tell you that I'm on your side.

I made some promises at the start of the book, and if you've played your part you'll have had some insights and "ahas" and have taken steps to build a solid foundation from which to really make progress that matters to you.

Perhaps there have been some miraculous seeming results produced in your life, and perhaps it seems like nothing has happened yet, nothing has shifted.

The nature of transformation is often seemingly no change no change no change, until in a moment the alchemy takes place. A caterpillar doesn't linearly understand the transformation into the butterfly. When do the cake ingredients become a cake?

These questions and ideas are now part of your toolset that you can draw on when you need or choose.

Let's get back to what matters, and now is the time when it's right to ask and consider, "What comes next? How will I apply this?"

Insights / Distinctions:

The World Quest™

What if there was an opportunity – a quest – that only reveals itself once we individually and collectively get to a certain point.

A Quest that would really matter, but we don't get to even know about it until we're ready. Why would that be the case? Well not to distract, confuse or frustrate us until we're have the capacity and capabilities to take it on.

We see this in computer games, where they don't start the real game until you've completed the tutorials.

Many challenges and quests in life can be completed individually.

They can be completed all more easily with guidance from wise mentors, friends, and family.

Learning to move and to communicate are some we all go through.

There are many that despite any book, training or support we still have to face alone.

What if The World Quest™ requires us coming together and really collaborating. Shifting our focus from survival and ego individually to something bigger.

Humanity is good at forming clans and tribes. Operating for our collective enlightened self-interest has so far eluded us in recorded history.

We're describing not a dictatorial chase for a flag, but something far distinct.

In any real quest there is a positive transformation to those on the search that is more profound than any could ever imagine.

What if there was such a quest?

What if it was your greatest adventure, just waiting for you to step up and take it on?

What if who you would become as you start, explore, and help complete this quest is even more amazing than your imagination could dream up?

What if it really will take all of us to Make The Difference™?

At times I thought I glimpsed it with such clarity and seen how the puzzle pieces could come together and have us all complete. Yet today we seem as a species not to have even started. When I am really present to this it can be very daunting and even distressing. On the good days it can be inspiring to imagine what could unfold.

If you were designing The World Quest™ and in charge of its goals and measures for completion, what would you design? What would you include?

For myself, I would have the basics included for all humanity. I describe these as:

- Every Mouth Fed – with nutritious high vibrational food.
- Every Thirst Quenched – with healthy clean fresh drinking water.
- Every Wound Healed – all internal and external wounds healed.

I believe that it's not until we as a collective reach these three basics consistently and with certainty that we can really start to explore the wider questions of what could really matter to us all.

It is also true for me that as each person, who is able, steps up and gains greater clarity and is able to build a world that works for them – a world that matters to them – with real integrity and abundance, we all get closer to that quest being complete.

I believe in a true WinWinWin, and that as each person increases their capacity for clarity, their ability to communicate, and efficiency at creating ethically that we all get a win.

I'm reminded as I write this of the Chinese story of Heaven and Hell, where both worlds are the same apart from in Heaven people feed in each other and in Hell people only try and feed themselves.

What would it take for you to be complete – really complete – so that you can from a place of abundance focus on what really matters to you?

Would it take any more for you to be able to help others to find their own clarity to focus on what matters to them too?

Perhaps just seeing you living with clarity and purpose would be enough?

Just as when someone gives us jigsaw puzzle with many pieces, we can find a way to put it together if we take the time to, so too I believe will be our journey with The World Quest™.

Sometimes we find pivotal pieces, dots that clearly connect together. At other times it can feel like looking for a needle in a haystack in a typhoon.

Perhaps the picture the pieces of our lives can create isn't as fixed as we think, and perhaps we get to make a say in it more than we imagine.

Perhaps there is no picture until we choose what really matters to us.

Perhaps nothing matters until we say so.

How do you feel about the idea of The World Quest™?

What did this exploration bring up for you?

Starting Points

When considering what really matters to us, it can be useful to consider what others who have gone before have defined as their meaning and as what matters to them.

Universally, some things that people often say matter include:

1. **Basic human needs:** Access to food, water, shelter, and healthcare are fundamental necessities for everyone's well-being and survival.
2. **Human rights:** Respect for individual rights and freedoms, such as freedom of speech, equality, and dignity, are essential for a just and fair society.
3. **Environmental stewardship:** Taking care of our planet and its resources is crucial for the well-being of current and future generations.
4. **Empathy and compassion:** Understanding and caring for others fosters a sense of community and helps create a more harmonious world.
5. **Education:** Access to quality education empowers individuals and societies to thrive and progress.
6. **Peace and security:** Stability and safety are fundamental for people to live fulfilling lives.
7. **Health and well-being:** Physical and mental health are essential for a fulfilling life and the ability to contribute positively to society.
8. **Cultural preservation:** Valuing and preserving diverse cultures enriches humanity and fosters mutual understanding.

These are some of the universal values and concerns that are significant across different cultures and societies.

As I share this book The Global Goals remain some of the objectives that governments have come together to declare as what matters.

Use these ideas as starting points for exploration and inquiry.

However just because something is held to be true by many people and for a long time doesn't mean it's "TRUE", nor has to matter for you.

You get to be in the pilot seat of your life and "try on" different orientations and notice the ripple effects they have in your results, experience of life and the world.

What insight and ideas have arisen from considering these starting points?

Action Steps

It can be very important to take what we learn and bring it into action.

Some would even say nothing happens until you take action. I don't want to force you into one method or another here, but there are many approaches we can share and will in the bonus resources and over time. I also believe that as your clarity increases, and you commit to moving more and more from Chaos To Clarity™ you will identify areas you want to optimise and be better prepared to ask for specific help.

Finding out what really matters can be a deeply personal and subjective process, as what matters most to one person may not be the same as what matters most to another. I recommend you start to journal and inquire alone, and in time with people you trust and respect.

However, here are some general steps you can take to help you identify what really matters to you:

Reflect on your values: Your values are the principles that guide your behaviour and decision-making. Spend some time reflecting on what values are most important to you, such as honesty, compassion, freedom, integrity, or justice.

Consider your passions and interests: Think about the things that excite you and bring you joy. What activities or hobbies do you enjoy doing? What subjects do you love learning about? Your passions and interests can give you clues about what really matters to you. Not just from what you're doing on the surface but the underlying states of being you experience in the process.

Think about your goals: What do you want to achieve in your life? What kind of person do you want to be? Setting goals can help you clarify what you want to focus on and what really matters to you. Think about the balance of Goal A vs Goal B. Which goals would you give up for the others? How many of the goals are about fixing something? How many are about yourself? How many are about others? How many are in your control to complete?

Consider your relationships: The people in your life can have a big impact on what matters to you. Think about the people you care about and the relationships that are important to you. What values and qualities do you admire in those people? Are you making time for what matters? Do those people know they matter, and that you really care?

Reflect on your experiences: Your life experiences can shape your perspective on what matters. Think about the moments that have had the biggest impact on you and what you learned from them. What experiences could you curate to expand your clarity and depth of understanding of what matters? Often helping others has this effect.

Schedule Your Success: Nothing in life seems to happen without some time – even if it's a microsecond or a few minutes. This is a key tenent of The Merlin Method™. It's powerful to schedule now a time to re-read / review this book and your notes. This could be in a few months or in a year. You may want to schedule a review of your priorities and experience of clarity – daily, weekly, monthly, quarterly, or annually. With modern electronic calendars you can easily setup repeating events. You may choose to schedule a day in nature away from the usual distractions to do this. Consider what you schedule and if it's aligned with what really matters. Also consider if you want to schedule time with your key partners, team members and stake holders for these reviews. These annual and strategic quarterly reviews can make all the difference.

Remember that what really matters to you may change over time as you grow and experience new things. It's okay – and in fact vital I believe – to reassess and adjust your priorities as needed.

Remember The Contexts

As you move forward now you can consider how these ideas and distinctions can be applied in any and all contexts. You may find some applications and insights to be universal and some very situational specific.

I have seen them applied with great results in every area and scale of life – from the simplicity of planning a day to the larger aspects of strategic planning for countries.

This book may have occurred as being very personal and in many ways it is. It also gives access to clarity in relation to business, legacy and any other context you care to imagine.

That's the beauty of distinctions and this approach.

Many of my clients and partners have been surprised how their greater personal clarity results in precessionary benefits in business. Many have come to my annual event or worked with me 1-1 and then a few months later raised capital, formed new business partnerships, launched new ventures, and been asked to speak at major events. These outcomes are all possible when you have greater clarity, get out of your own way, and allow yourself to engage with reality in new ways.

There are clearly different skills and tools that need to be applied tactically in business than in say making lunch for a friend. However, the ontological aspects that produce success I think are very aligned across all aspects of performance.

Some people find their standards raise – as you do one thing, so they say you do all things. Remember the metaphor of finally putting on clean glasses that are the right prescription. Everything will be clearer. You get to choose where you look at the stairs or the stars.

Also remember that almost everything unless it's really something you can accomplish by yourself is accomplished by and through communications and interactions with other people.

As you better understand yourself and you have acted in the past, and what motivates you and how you can perform optimally, there becomes the possibility for greater empathy and efficacy with others.

You might be surprised how many senior business, government or policy meetings are full of people who are stuck in Chaos and almost fighting for it. When you are able to come with the distinctions necessary to objectively move a person or project from Chaos To Clarity™ you can be a real asset.

In time I hope these ideas and this book will be shared more and perhaps we will have more and more real collaboration and actual teams working interdependently together with clarity optimally. I would love to see The World Quest™ complete in my lifetime.

As you move forward now look for opportunities to add to your insights from this book through their application in the real world. Record these in your journal and review them often. Your life can become your biggest learning tool.

For example, you can notice where Rule One, Rule Two or Rule Three are and are not being applied.

More importantly you'll now be better able to consider what really matters to you – not what others say should matter.

Final Thought

Much thanks for letting me share Chaos To Clarity™ with you.

I wish for you only the best, and I hope you've enjoyed this book and this journey with me. If you've got value, please let me know and pay it forward.

Wherever you're at in the world today and in your own life's journey, know that we all have the choice to keep taking things one breath at a time, one moment at a time, and in each moment have the choice to remember what really matters.

I also believe you'll see new opportunities to explore and act moving forward, and to do so in new ways.

In the good times, I hope you remain grateful and can acknowledge your good fortune. In the challenging times, always remember Nil Desperandum and that you matter.

Until next time, "Bon voyage et bonne chance."

Love,
Simon
X

Chapter 13

Top Priorities

Having clarity on your top priorities makes all the difference, and I've left space here in the book for you to consider and actual write out physically your Top Priorities.

Does the thought of writing with confidence in the book thrill you or challenge you?

Do you find yourself thinking what if they change? I'm not sure what they are?

Or…

Are you super clear right now about what your top priorities are?

Having a visual reminder is so important and the very act of documenting and writing for me has made all the difference.

When you get really clear and committed around your priorities you will take different actions.

One of the greatest business philosophers of recent times and a mentor to many who have led the personal and business development teachings of my time was Jim Rohn. Jim Rohn's mentor – Earl Shoaff – encouraged him to have documented goals and I would encourage you to do the same.

Having read through this book, and now understand more than ever the importance of having the clarity on what really matters to you – you will be better able to declare your Top Priorities.

What you declare as your priorities will also be more aligned with your whole.

It's also ok, to feel like.. I'm not clear yet.. and start to consider what they are.

I've been working with and teaching about priorities and prioritisation for decade, and there is still much to learn. I may even share a book on this subject in the future.

However for today I have deliberately given you spaces for just 3 choices.

What you choose to declare and document as your priorities is up to you.

Having just one clear real grounded priority can be better, but in life as we've seen there is often Chaos.

I would encourage to review what you declare as your top priorities quarterly, monthly, weekly, or even daily and this is where the Pause Stop Reset Journal can come in very useful.

I want you to know that there's also a power and momentum in having clear top priorities that are consistent and congruent for you that last over time. Especially as you share them with others you trust, and they come to support you in focussing on your top priorities and getting them complete.

P.S.

If you're concerned about writing in the book, that's ok and I would still encourage you to. I also know the value in having a copy you can print out and put up on a wall or whiteboard. So, you can find a pdf downloadable version on the online book bonus page which you're welcome to use time and again. You're welcome to share this download and the other bonuses with people you think it will help, in fact I would love you to.

The link for the bonuses is
www.ChaosToClarity.com/bookbonuses

P.S.

Just because there are 3 spaces doesn't mean you have to use them all.

If you find that really you have ONE Top priority and nothing else then write it boldly and clearly, and know you'll always have space if something else arises.

TOP PRIORITIES

1.

2.

3.

Chapter 14

Book Bonus Resources

I created an online portal to go alone with this book, and you can access it, as my gift, by going to www.ChaosToClarity.com/bookbonuses.

Here you'll find resources to inspire and help you on your journey from Chaos To Clarity™, including the downloadable pdf for your top priorities.

My intention is to keep adding to these online resources over time.

So, for now thank you for reading and being part of this journey and while the book is complete, our journey is just beginning.

I really do hope you'll take advantage of all the bonuses and opportunities that I've made available and put what you have learnt from this book into action.

A Reminder and Suggestion:

If you've gotten value, please share about it online and pay it forward and pass this book on to a friend.

Just selling a book was never my goal – making the difference is – and by sharing ideas and books with the people you care about I truly believe we can do that one person at a time.

The Strategic Alchemist™

For over two decades, Mr. Simon Hedley FCA has been the secret weapon of many well-known leaders, founders and thought leaders. Often due to confidentiality and non-disclosure agreements being known simply as Simon X.

For his inner circle of friends, clients and partners who really know him, he's known as **The Strategic Alchemist™** for his capacity to make things happen "as if by magic", and his ability to be and do what it takes to Make The Difference™ over decades and more.

He's been an ultimate connector of people and projects and helping them prepare and get complete, and over the decades inspired and birthed countless businesses, projects, and movements.

He knows the power and impact that being present, listening, asking a simple question, or making a suggestion can have in the moment and over time. Even if it seems as if nothing material happened at all. In fact, sometimes that's the best way to really make the difference.

He is committed to Making The Difference™ and Helping Good People Do Great Things™.

He founded **Simon X™** to provide strategic advisory and management services to creative entrepreneurs. Learn more at www.SimonX.com.

You can learn more about Simon and his professional background that includes Audit and Investment Banking at www.SimonHedley.com.

If you're committed to doing whatever it takes to make something happen, and are ready to really see what's possible, then learn how he works with founders and companies at www.TheStrategicAlchemist.com.

Your Invitation and Offer

If you've enjoyed this book and would like to explore what's really possible and get hands on help with implementing Chaos To Clarity™ and taking practical steps forward, then I'd love you to consider this invitation to learn more about a special offer that I have for you.

I talked and brainstormed with my partners and mentors how best to help those who want to connect and want my help in a real WinWinWin.

Because you've read the book and taken the time to do the work, I know you're committed to moving from Chaos To Clarity™, I also know it's really valuable to get an informed outside perspective.

I really love working with people like you and so I'm prepared to make you an incredible offer that I think may be what it takes to make the difference for you.

To learn more about this invitation and offer please go to:

www.ChaosToClarity.com/offer

Your Invitation and Offer

BV - #0022 - 210823 - C0 - 216/138/11 [13] - CB - 9781914155031 - Gloss Lamination